ARISTOTLE ON THE ART OF FICTION

An English translation of
ARISTOTLE'S *POETICS*
with an introductory essay and
explanatory notes

by

L. J. POTTS

*Fellow of Queens' College and
University Lecturer in English in the
University of Cambridge*

CAMBRIDGE
AT THE UNIVERSITY PRESS
1959

PUBLISHED BY
THE SYNDICS OF THE CAMBRIDGE UNIVERSITY PRESS

Bentley House, 200 Euston Road, London, N.W. 1
American Branch: 32 East 57th Street, New York 22, N.Y.

First edition 1953
Reprinted 1959

Printed in Great Britain at the University Press, Cambridge
(Brooke Crutchley, University Printer)

PREFACE TO THE SECOND IMPRESSION

In preparing this book for a second impression I have revised it extensively. In particular I have re-written the note on Aristotle's use of the term KATHOLOU in the *Poetics* (pages 71–3) and have so far overcome my dislike of the word 'universal' as to use it in the important passage on page 29. I have also made two additions to the bibliography.

The critics and reviewers of the first edition were good enough to make many suggestions about vocabulary and phrasing; almost every change I have made is in response to an objection from one or another of them. I owe them a large debt for encouragement and practical help; it would be invidious to select particular persons for special thanks. But I cannot let this occasion pass without putting on record my grief at the untimely death of Humphry House and paying tribute to his unique achievements as a scholar and critic.

L. J. P.

QUEENS' COLLEGE, CAMBRIDGE

December 1958

CONTENTS

Introduction   *page* 1

Short Bibliography   16

ON THE ART OF FICTION   17

Notes

   A. Incompleteness of the *Poetics*   62

   B. The definition of poetry   64

   C. The fable   69

   D. Aesthetic values   75

   E. References to Greek literature and drama
      in the *Poetics*   82

Index   89

INTRODUCTION

THIS is not the place for a full account of the influence of
the *Poetics* on literature; and indeed it seems impossible
that such an account should ever be written. We know
nothing about the first seventeen or eighteen hundred years
of its existence, except a few bare facts; and even some of
those are deduced. That it was written by Aristotle is not
questioned. He did not publish it; it was a small fragment
of the mass of knowledge and thought accumulated by him
and studied by his pupils. There is no evidence of its
influence in the pre-Roman period. The poet Horace knew
something of its contents, probably at second hand. In the
third century A.D., Diogenes Laertius, the biographer of
the Greek philosophers, included it in his list of Aristotle's
works, stating that it consisted of *two* books. About three
centuries later it was translated into Syriac; and about the
tenth century that Syriac version was in its turn translated
into Arabic. This Arabic version still exists, and is the
earliest authentic (but very garbled) record of the contents
of the *Poetics*. In the eleventh century the manuscript upon
which our knowledge of the Greek text chiefly depends
was written by a Byzantine scribe. Then, somehow, in the
fifteenth century, the Greek text became well known in
Italy; several copies made in that century have survived,
and a Latin translation was printed in 1498.

What part the *Poetics* played in preserving the Greek
literary tradition through the Middle Ages cannot therefore be determined. Some part it must have played
indirectly. Even our own literature provides a small

piece of evidence; for Chaucer's well-known definition of tragedy:

> Tragedie is to seyn a certeyn storie,
> As olde bookes maken us memorie,
> Of *hym that stood in greet prosperitee*,
> And is yfallen *out of heigh degree*
> Into myserie, and endeth wrecchedly.
>
> (*Canterbury Tales*, Monk's Prologue.)

contains fragments of a sentence in Chapter 13 of the *Poetics* ('the kind of man who neither is distinguished for excellence and virtue, nor comes to grief on account of baseness and vice, but on account of some error; *a man of great reputation and prosperity*, like Oedipus and Thyestes and *conspicuous people of such families as theirs*': 33.22–7). But during the years when the Latin world of the west was cut off from the Greek world of the east the treatise itself was not known in Europe. It is unlikely that much use would have been made of it if it had been.[1]

The Italian scholars of the sixteenth century were enormously interested in the *Poetics*, and early in the century dramatists began to follow Aristotle's guidance in writing their tragedies. But before English writers became familiar with it, it had been assimilated into the mass of theory about literature, and poetry in particular, that formed one of the main channels of the Renaissance. It has to be admitted that, speaking quantitatively, the greater part of the influence of the *Poetics* on our writers has consisted in unverified beliefs that Aristotle said this or that, which he did not say. The spurious rule of the Three Unities is the most famous of these un-Aristotelian accretions.

It is sometimes supposed that the influence of the *Poetics* was at its height during the ages of Dryden and

[1] For the early history of the *Poetics*, see Bywater (Introduction, pp. xxiii–xxvi); Margoliouth (Chapter II, pp. 77–9); Lane Cooper (Chapters 7–12).

2

Pope. So it might seem from Pope's beautifully written tribute in the *Essay on Criticism*:

> The mighty Stagirite first left the shore,
> Spread all his sails, and durst the deeps explore;
> He steer'd securely, and discover'd far
> Led by the light of the Maeonian star.
> Poets, a race long unconfin'd and free,
> Still fond and proud of savage liberty,
> Receiv'd his laws; and stood convinc'd 'twas fit
> Who conquer'd Nature, should preside o'er Wit.

But, setting aside the reverence for Homer, which was a real stimulus to the Augustan poets, there is nothing of the *Poetics* in this, and nothing in the rest of the *Essay* except superficialities that Pope could have gleaned (and probably did glean) from Boileau and Horace. His predecessor Dryden was too wholeheartedly concerned with the special problems of the English poet in the late seventeenth century to pay serious attention to the *general* principles of poetic composition at all. The remarks on Rymer, which Johnson printed at the end of his Life of Dryden, illustrate this; they contain the only profound observation that Dryden made about Aristotle, a purely negative one, which he could have made without reading a word of the *Poetics*:

> It is not enough that Aristotle has said so; for Aristotle drew his models of tragedy from Sophocles and Euripides; and if he had seen ours, might have changed his mind.

Johnson himself was by temperament an Aristotelian; he had an encyclopedic and at the same time truly logical mind; and he was not only a better scholar but a much better philosopher than either Dryden or Pope. In his Preface to Shakespeare he shows that he understood the principles of imitation and unity better than the orthodox critics. He had surely read the *Poetics*; but his first principles for poetry are different from Aristotle's, and the only explicit

reference to Aristotle in the Preface is almost off-hand
though exceedingly apt. Speaking of Shakespeare's
observance of the Unity of Action, he writes:

He has not, indeed, an intrigue regularly perplexed and
regularly unravelled: he does not endeavour to hide his
design only to discover it, for this is seldom the order of
real events, and Shakespeare is the poet of nature: But
his plan has commonly what Aristotle requires, a beginning,
a middle, and an end; one event is concatenated with
another, and the conclusion follows by easy consequence.

The Greek critic who most inspired the Augustans was
Longinus, not Aristotle; and, though by Johnson's time
the *Poetics* was about to enter on its second phase of
influence in this country, I have had to go to the ages of
Shakespeare and Wordsworth to find weightier evidence
of the impression the *Poetics* has made on our leading
critics. In the quotations that follow the italics are mine.

SIR PHILIP SIDNEY:

Truly Aristotle himself in his discourse of Poesie *plainly
determineth this question*, saying that Poetry is 'Philo-
sophoteron' and 'Spoudaioteron', that is to say, it is more
philosophical and more studiously serious than history.
His reason is, because Poesie dealeth with 'Katholou',
that is to say with the universal consideration, and the
history with 'Kathekaston', the particular: 'Now,' saith
he, 'the universal weighs what is fit to be said or done,
either in likelihood or necessity (which the Poesie con-
sidereth in his imposed names), and the particular only
marks whether Alcibiades did or suffered this or that.' Thus
far Aristotle: which reason of his (*as all his*) is most full
of reason. (*Apology for Poesy, c.* 1583.)

BEN JONSON:

Aristotle was *the first accurate Critic, and truest Judge*, nay
the greatest Philosopher, the world ever had: for he noted
the vices of all knowledges, in all creatures, and out of

4

many men's perfections in a Science he formed still one Art. So he taught us two Offices together, *how we ought to judge rightly of others, and what we ought to imitate specially in ourselves.* (? *c.* 1635, from *Timber.*)

COLERIDGE:

I adopt with full faith the principle of Aristotle that poetry, as poetry, is essentially ideal, that it avoids and excludes all accident: that its apparent individualities of rank, character, or occupation, must be representative of a class: and that the persons of poetry must be clothed with generic attributes, with the common attributes of the class: not with such as one gifted individual might possibly possess, but such as from his situation it is most probable beforehand that he would possess. (*Biographia Literaria,* 1817.)

MATTHEW ARNOLD:

We all naturally take pleasure, says Aristotle, in any imitation or representation whatever: this is the basis of our love of Poetry: and we take pleasure in them, he adds, because all knowledge is naturally agreeable to us; not to the philosopher only, but to mankind at large. Every representation *therefore* which is consistently drawn *may be supposed* to be interesting, inasmuch as it gratifies this natural interest in knowledge of all kinds. What is not interesting is that which does not add to our knowledge of any kind; that which is vaguely conceived and loosely drawn; a representation which is general, indeterminate, and faint, instead of being particular, precise, and firm. (Preface to *Poems,* 1853.)

Add, as a splendid curiosity, WORDSWORTH'S tribute to the tradition:

Aristotle, *I have been told,* has said that Poetry is the most philosophic of all writing: it is so: its object is truth, not individual and local, but general, and operative; not standing upon external testimony, but carried alive into the heart by passion; truth which is its own testimony, which gives competence and confidence to the tribunal to which it appeals, and receives them from the same tribunal. (Preface to *Lyrical Ballads*, Second Edition, 1800.)

And even as late as 1925 a young and original critic could still write:

Although historians of aesthetics are sometimes pleased to present their facts as though they represented a progress from cruder to more refined opinion, from ignorance to wisdom, there is no sound basis for the procedure. Aristotle was at least as clearly and fully aware of the relevant facts and as adequate in his explanations as any later inquirers. (I. A. Richards, *Principles of Literary Criticism*, Chapter x, pp. 71-2, n.)

How far the authors I have quoted, and the others, understood the purport of Aristotle's generalizations and precepts correctly, or each for his own purposes distorted them, is another question; or rather a series of questions, which constitute the greater part of the history of literary theory in England. Sidney had read at least some parts of the *Poetics* closely; he quotes accurately and expounds his quotations with care. There is no sign in the *Apology* of rebellion against Aristotle's authority, only of admiration modestly accorded to an intellectual pre-eminence 'out-topping knowledge'. But Jonson was a disciple of Bacon and admired the *Advancement of Learning* without reserve; and elsewhere in *Timber* he quotes the famous passage in which Bacon had slighted the Schoolmen and their master Aristotle. The *Poetics*, however, had not been annexed by scholastic philosophy, and therefore Jonson and his contemporaries could annex it for their own ends without scruple; and Aristotle's predominant interest in the psychology of the poet and his audience was particularly congenial to a generation fascinated by psychological speculation. Jonson himself was a conscientious scholar, inclined more than any of our other great writers to be guided by critical principles in his own poetry and drama, and he came as near to a correct interpretation of Aristotle's general theory of poetry as any of them has. He saw clearly that by poetry Aristotle meant *fiction*: the embodiment of a philosophy of life in stories or situations such as we meet in the real world except that they are more consistent, being free from both the inert superficialities that signify nothing, and the occasional contradictory happenings that appear for the moment to invalidate general truths. To this conception of poetry Jonson was faithful, above all in his comedies, which are almost as far as possible in the world of fiction from Spenser's *Faerie Queene*, the poem to which Sidney's *Apology* looks forward. Thus within a few years the *Poetics* was invoked to justify two opposite conceptions of poetry—high idealist allegory and naturalistic fable.

A somewhat similar contradiction appears in my quotations from Coleridge and Arnold. Coleridge insists that the apparent individualities of poetry must be representative of a class, whereas Arnold argues that the representation should not be general but particular. Yet they both appeal to the authority of Aristotle. The contradiction is perhaps more apparent than real, since Coleridge is referring rather to the subject-matter of poetry and Arnold rather to the finished product; still, they use the testimony of Aristotle to justify theses of opposite tendency. And with these later writers the question arises: Why did they rely on Aristotle? The popularity of the *Poetics* among scholars and poets in the sixteenth and seventeenth centuries was chiefly due to an accident. They happened to discover it when they were most feeling the need of a coherent tradition to work in, and especially of a serious and comprehensive key to the great Greek poets, to give them a high and humane standard by which to judge themselves and each other, and to show them more clearly what they must do in order to emulate or surpass the great literatures of antiquity. But by the beginning of the nineteenth century the doctrines of the *Poetics* had lost their freshness and many of them had been challenged or even rejected; and two such sophisticated writers as Coleridge and Arnold cannot any longer have shared Ben Jonson's naïve faith in the finality of Aristotle's answers to all possible questions about the end of poetry and the best means to that end.

It is now clear that the *Poetics* has had a second phase of popularity in England, distinct from its first phase. This second phase perhaps began when Coleridge revived and reinterpreted some of Aristotle's leading principles in the *Biographia Literaria*; and it culminated in Butcher's translation and explanatory essays, and Bywater's great edition with its accompanying translation. It centred more and more in the Universities. It was a by-product of the literary education of the Victorians, which was based on the thorough study and imitation of a few great classical Greek and Latin authors. It was natural therefore that as the academic interest in critical theory heightened at the end of the nineteenth and the beginning of the twentieth century, scholars should have taken an increasing interest in the only comprehensive philosophical theory of literature that has survived from Graeco-Roman antiquity. But it was a different kind of interest from Ben Jonson's, for example; and the admiration that accompanied it did not assume that Aristotle's answers were the right ones, but only (to quote Mr F. L. Lucas,[1] writing in 1928) that he asked the right questions.

A quarter of a century has passed since Mr Lucas and Professor Richards gave their somewhat different reasons for still retaining the *Poetics* as a live document in the

[1] *Tragedy*, revised edition, p. 12.

8

corpus of literary theory. But latterly new writers have given a new look to our poetry, and revealed unfamiliar aspects of our poetic tradition—and under the term 'poetry' I include, as any interpreter of Aristotle must, the art of fiction in narrative or dramatic form. The old reasons for studying the *Poetics* seem inadequate. I believe there are other reasons, at least equally potent.

The chief importance of Aristotle's theory of poetry lies in two principles, which at the same time are our chief sources of difficulty: that poetry is a species of imitation, and that the myth (rather than character or language) is the essence of tragedy. As imitation is the first principle on which the whole of the *Poetics* is founded, I will take it first.

Plato, who seldom in his dialogues simplifies any human activity, never goes so far as to lay it down that all poetry is a sort of imitation; but he clearly regarded poets with suspicion as incorrigible imitators. Moreover, to judge from the *Cratylus*, he thought that language itself is essentially imitative, which makes it difficult to maintain that he drew a fundamental distinction between imitative and any other kind of poetry. On the other hand, his treatment of imitation is often only half serious, as when he insinuates that Homer was not qualified to write the *Iliad* because he had no training in strategy. But Aristotle leaves no loophole; he states categorically that the poet is a poet by virtue of imitating. It seems clear that for him all poetry was essentially a kind of fiction; and the *Poetics* is best understood as a treatise on fiction. Expounders of Aristotle's theory have attempted to make it clearer by using other words instead of 'imitate': 'represent', or 're-produce', or even 'express'. But these words, though they remove some possible misunderstandings, create others. The radical idea is embodying another nature, identifying oneself with it, and acting as it would act. That

9

is what Aristotle means when he says that dancers imitate characters by the rhythm of their postures. Or it can take the form of evocative creation, as in magical arts—the waxen images that their makers melted or stuck pins into were not in intention portraits, but *substitutes*. It is also possible to imitate a whole scene or story, involving several persons, by (as we say) 'living' it. Essentially imitation is not what Plato professed to see in it, an easy way of deluding the senses of the public; it is what in rather misleading modern parlance we call 'creative imagination'. The striking paragraph at the beginning of Chapter 17 tells the dramatist to visualise his scenes, and sympathise with all his speakers. This is the way not only to avoid blunders but to 'find the right thing in its most vivid form'; and it is chiefly because of the superior vividness of drama that Aristotle places it above narrative fiction in his last chapter.

So far, then, from watering down his notion of imitation, or dismissing it as a crude and dated theory of poetry, I plead for its reinstatement. It is a good theory, and of more value to us nowadays than, for example, the theory of poetry as a means of self-expression. Self-expression is certainly a strong motive in all works of art, but it is not a specifically artistic motive; it is no less active in love, in the battle of life, and indeed in all our doings. Baudelaire's dry comment on Juvenal's famous 'facit indignatio versum'—that the world is full of very angry persons, who are not always good poets—is a just criticism of the notion that the *end* of art is self-expression.

Aristotle differs similarly from Plato in his attitude to 'Fable' or Myth. That Plato himself made fables and used them to reinforce the drama and dialectic of his dialogues has obscured this; but famous as they are, his fables are bloodless things. His great myth was his other world of

Ideas, a myth of another kind, more akin to mathematics than to poetry. As for the traditional mythology of the Greek poets, he surely felt its power, but his principles forced him to stigmatize it as a bundle of degrading lies. Not so Aristotle. For him the myths were a truthful revelation of the importance of human action.[1] The Fable is the life and soul of tragedy, because 'our end is a certain kind of doing, not a personal quality', and it is our doings, and not our characters, that make us happy or unhappy. At first sight this argument seems naïve. It is moreover contrary to the Christian tradition, which does not separate being from doing but teaches that they are complementary. But it is the pagan morality of doing rather than being that gives to both the Homeric epic and Greek tragedy their characteristic temper of heroic fatalism, and Aristotle is right to insist on the poetic value of the Greek myths.[2] True, when he tries to find explanations for the re-use of a few old stories in tragedy after tragedy, his argument misses the main point; he even seems to think it might be better if dramatists made up their own stories. Perhaps that was because in his day the traditional mythology had lost its hold on the people. But he shows his understanding of myth in a more general sense by harping so insistently on Probability and Necessity. The essence of a myth, for Aristotle, is that it is consistent; within it the sequence of events is necessary or probable, and people act according to their characters. Outside myth it is not always so; to any one man many things happen, and some of them do not make any sort of unity. What makes poetry philosophical and valuable is that it tells the sort of thing that *would* happen, not everything that does happen.

The word 'philosophical' in that crucial sentence in Chapter 9 is the most astonishing word in the *Poetics*. Of

[1] See Note C. 2, p. 70. [2] In Chapter 13.

course both Plato and Aristotle believed in a Cosmos—
a fitness of all things to the sum of things. The immense
value of Plato's philosophy was that it endowed 'all
thinking things, all objects of all thought' with a comprehensive significance, at a time (like ours) when most
educated men had ceased to be able to accept the documents
of their traditional religion as historically true. At such
times no literary criticism is of any value except the
criticism of philosophers; for all true philosophers see that
life makes sense, and without that vision criticism de-
generates into arbitrary rules, running into more and more
lifeless details. Consequently Plato's literary criticism has
a high value at the present time. But Plato was driven to
the conclusion that poetry, and indeed all literature, was
a mere game—a noble game perhaps, but pernicious if it
was taken seriously. That is one of the positions that
a twentieth-century critic can sincerely take up: a worth-
while position, therefore. On the other hand Aristotle,
because of his different attitude to imitation and myth,
came to the opposite conclusion about poetry: that it is not
false or at best insignificant, but *philosophical* and *of high
value*. And substantially one must take up one or the other
of these two positions.

The *Poetics* belongs to the last period of Aristotle's career
(335–323 B.C.), when he was teaching and lecturing in the
Lyceum at Athens. Athens had long since ceased to be
a great power; the leadership of Hellas had passed to the
kings of Macedon, and while Aristotle was mapping out
his system of knowledge and thought his former pupil
Alexander the Great was pursuing an only less ambitious
scheme of eastern conquest. The body of poetry of which
Aristotle speaks in the *Poetics* was therefore already old.
But it was not a dead literature; Aristotle not only

generalizes from it, but also gives advice and injunctions to those who were still adding to it. Since we possess no complete Greek tragedy written after 405 B.C. we cannot test his generalizations inductively; but fortunately for our understanding of his theory, his favourite examples were old, and several of them have survived.

Aristotle's chief bent was for natural science, but he was also a logician, psychologist, moralist, metaphysician, and student of political and social history. He taught, to the most advanced standard then reached, most of the subjects studied at a university nowadays. His contribution to literary criticism—the *Rhetoric* and the *Poetics*—is a small part of his critical survey of Greek social life; and the *Rhetoric* is much the larger (though also much the less important) of the two. One would scarcely notice the *Poetics* among his surviving works unless one were looking for it; and indeed its preservation is something of a miracle. Yet without it his survey would have been incomplete. Poetry played a prominent part in the life of the Athenians; Homer was their Bible, and Aristotle's master, Plato, had given much attention to poetry in his moral and political teaching. In the Tenth Book of the *Republic* Plato challenges any lover of poetry who is not himself a poet to answer his charges against the poets; and Aristotle was probably taking up that challenge in the *Poetics*, if he had not already done so in his early dialogue *On the Poets*, which like all his other dialogues has perished.

It has been my aim to provide the English reader who is interested in the theory of literature and knows little or no Greek, with the nearest approximation to a plain text of the *Poetics* that I could achieve in our different language. My version therefore differs in kind and intention from Bywater's, which was originally printed as a guide to the reading of the Greek. I have followed the Greek text as closely as I could, except where literalness would have led to inaccuracy or a grossly un-English idiom; and I have only very rarely expanded the sense. Substantial additions —words or phrases that involve more than a difference between Greek and English idiom—I have marked by enclosing them in ⟨pointed brackets⟩. Where the thought itself is obscure I have tried to reproduce it as it stands; where the Greek will bear more than one sense I have chosen the sense that seems to me most probable and expressed it as unambiguously as I can. I have based my translation on Bywater's great edition, and I had advanced some way before I realized that I could not evade the onus of textual criticism; a translator must believe in the text he is translating, and though Bywater is by far the most judicious of the modern editors his judgement cannot have been infallible. Moreover, not a little work has been done on the text since 1909. I have therefore compared his doubtful readings with those of Butcher, Margoliouth, Rostagni, and Gudeman, all four of whom I believe to be once or twice right where they differ from Bywater. I have seldom discussed the merits of alternative readings at length; but I have marked the most important places where the Greek text is corrupt or doubtful with asterisks at the *beginning and end* of the passage, and when I have followed a different reading from Bywater's I have usually quoted his version in a footnote. In deference to a difficulty sometimes felt by English readers I have marked some of the vowels in Greek words either long (as in Hēgēmon) or short (as in Nicochăres).

I have not made any attempt to provide a full commentary, believing with Doctor Johnson that such commentaries are more often a hindrance than a help to the unlearned reader. But a minimum of explanation is necessary, and I have tried to concentrate as much of it as possible in the five short notes at the end of the book, on general topics. It would forestall some difficulty and misunderstanding to read quickly through the first four of them and the first section of Note E (pp. 62–84) before beginning to read the translation. Aristotle's literary and critical vocabulary presents special difficulties to the translator; I have tried to explain his most important terms in the notes and by means of the index—see, for example, the entries under 'Fable' (p. 90) and 'Universal' (p. 93). The translation can, I hope, be read without much attention to the footnotes, which are intended for those who have reached the stage of studying the *Poetics* carefully in detail. The marginal headings are an addition of my own; I found that they helped me to follow the development of Aristotle's analysis, and although they have no authority I have inserted them to give a similar help to the reader. He may ignore or modify them at his discretion. For convenience of reference I have numbered the lines on each page of the translation. In making exact references I have given page and line; thus, for example, **29**.5 means page 29 line 5.

The short bibliography may serve as an acknowledgement of my chief debts. My friend and colleague at Queens', John Trevaskis, generously spent many hours on my translation when I had finished it, and he has given me the benefit of numerous valuable criticisms and suggestions, especially about the textual problems; but for any errors or defects I am solely responsible. I am deeply grateful to the Syndics of the Cambridge University Press for their unfailing courtesy and wise advice in discussing the form this little book should take.

SHORT BIBLIOGRAPHY

INGRAM BYWATER, *Aristotle on the Art of Poetry*, 1909. [Introduction, text, translation, and commentary.] 'Bywater.'

do., with a preface by Gilbert Murray, 1920. [The translation published separately.]

do., ed. W. Hamilton Fyfe, 1940. [The translation re-published, with an introduction and explanatory notes by Sir W. Hamilton Fyfe.]

S. H. BUTCHER, *Aristotle's Theory of Poetry and Fine Art*, 3rd edition, 1902. [Text, translation, and critical essays.] 'Butcher.'

D. S. MARGOLIOUTH, *The Poetics of Aristotle*, 1911. [Introduction, text, translation, and Latin translation of the Arabic version.] 'Margoliouth.'

W. HAMILTON FYFE, *Aristotle's Poetics* (Loeb Classical Library), 1927. [Text, translation, and commentary.]

LANE COOPER, *The Poetics of Aristotle* ('Our Debt to Greece and Rome'), 1924. [Essay on the meaning and influence of the *Poetics*.] 'Lane Cooper.'

F. L. LUCAS, *Tragedy*: Serious drama in relation to Aristotle's *Poetics*, revised edition, 1957. [Critical interpretation.]

HUMPHRY HOUSE, *Aristotle's Poetics*, 1956. [Controversial interpretation.]

THEODOR GOMPERZ, *Greek Thinkers*, volume iv, translated by G. G. Berry, 1912. [Aristotle.]

W. D. ROSS, *Aristotle*, 5th edition, revised 1949. ['An account of the main features of Aristotle's philosophy.'] 'Ross.'

ON THE ART OF
FICTION

CHAPTER 1. Let us talk of the art of poetry as a whole, *Title*
and its different species with the particular force of each of
them; how the fables must be put together if the poetry is to
be well formed; also what are its elements and their different
5 qualities; and all other matters pertaining to the subject.

To begin in the proper order, at the beginning. The making *First*
of epics and of tragedies, and also comedy, and the art of *Premise*
the dithyramb, and most flute[1] and lyre art, all have this in
common, that they are imitations. But they differ from one
10 another in three respects: the different kinds of medium in
which they imitate, the different objects they imitate, and the
different manner in which they imitate (when it does differ).

Just as some people imitate many things in colour and *Medium*
outline, depicting them either by a deliberate technique or
15 by trial and error, and others imitate by the voice, so the
arts I have mentioned all do their imitating in one or more
of the following media—rhythm, language, and music. The
arts of the flute and lyre use only music and rhythm, and so
does any other art that has a similar force, for example the
20 art of the pipes. Ballet imitates by sheer rhythm, without
music; for dancers too imitate characters and experiences
and doings by the rhythm of their postures. *Epic poetry:
by language alone: prose or verse: verse either in a mixture
of metres, or using only one kind (which is what it
25 happens to have done up to the present).*[2]

[1] Cf. Chapter 26 (59.17–19). See also Note B, p. 67.
[2] Or, according to Bywater's reading: 'There is further an art
which imitates by language alone, without harmony, in prose or in

(N.B. We have no term to denote the class that includes the farces of Sophron and Xenarchus, and Socratic dialogues; nor should we have one even if the imitating were done in iambic trimeters or elegiacs or any other metre. People append the term 'poetry' to the metre, 5 distinguishing for example between 'elegiac poets' and 'epic poets'. They class them, not as poets in virtue of the act of imitating, but according to the metre used; even if some one produces a work on medicine or music in verse form, they are in the habit of calling him a poet. But Homer 10 and Empedocles have nothing in common except their metre; and therefore, while it is correct to call the former a poet, the latter should be called a scientist rather than a poet. Again, even if some one did his imitating in a mixture of all the metres, as Chaerēmon actually did in 15 his *Centaur*—a rhapsody in a mixture of all the metres—he would have to be classed simply as a poet. That is the way in which we ought to distinguish between writers.)

Now there are some kinds of imitation that use all the traditional media, such as rhythm, melody, and verse: 20 dithyrambic and nomic poetry and tragedy and comedy do so. But they differ from one another in that the first two use all these media together, while the second two use them successively. So much for the differences between the arts depending on the media in which they do their 25 imitating.

Object CHAPTER 2. When the imitators imitate the doings of people, the people in the imitation must be either high or low;[1] the characters almost always follow this line

verse, and if in verse, either in some one or in a plurality of metres. This form of imitation is to this day without a name.' But all the Greek manuscripts have the reading that I have translated. See Note B, pp. 68–9.

[1] See Note D, p. 77.

exclusively, for all men differ in character according to their degree of goodness or badness. They must therefore be either above our norm, or below it, or normal; as, in painting, Polygnōtus depicted superior, Pauson inferior,
5 and Dionysius normal, types. It is clear that each variant of imitation that I have mentioned will have these differences, and as the object imitated varies in this way so the works will differ. Even in the ballet, and in flute and lyre music, these dissimilarities can occur; and in the art that uses
10 prose, or verse without music, as Homer depicted superior types, Cleophon normal types, and Hēgēmon of Thasos (the first writer of parodies) and Nicochăres (the author of the *Deiliad*) inferior types; so also in the dithyramb and the nome imitations may vary *as the Cyclopses of Timothěŭs and
15 Philoxěnus varied.*[1] This is the difference that marks tragedy out from comedy; comedy is inclined to imitate persons below the level of our world, tragedy persons above it.

CHAPTER 3. Again, a third difference between these *Manner* arts is the manner in which each of these objects can be
20 imitated. For given the same medium and the same object, one can imitate partly by narration and partly by dramatic dialogue (as Homer does); or one can speak invariably in one's own person; or one can use actors to imitate the whole thing as though they were living it themselves.
25 The imitation, then, differs in these three respects, as we *Summary* said at the beginning: in medium, in object, and in manner. *of Classi-* Thus Sophocles would be in one respect in the same class of *fications* imitators as Homer, for both imitate high people; but in another respect in the same class as Aristophanes, for they
30 both imitate by means of actors in a performance.

1 Or, according to Margoliouth: 'e.g. the Earths and Cyclopes of Timotheus and Philoxenus.' The manuscript is probably corrupt here, but the general sense is clear.

Etymo-logical Digres-sion (Some say this is the origin of the term *drama*, from the verb DRĀN (to perform). Hence the Dorians claim both tragedy and comedy. (The Megarians lay claim to comedy: those in the mother country on the assumption that it belonged to the date when their city became a democracy, and the Megarian colonists in Sicily because the poet Epicharmus, who was a countryman of theirs, was much earlier than Chionïdes and Magnes. Some of the Dorians in the Peloponnese also lay claim to tragedy.) Their argument is etymological. They say their name for a satellite village is KŌMĒ, whereas the Athenian name is DEMOS; for they derive the word comedy not from KŌMOS (revel), but from KOME, because the comedians left the city, where they were looked down on, and toured the villages. And their word for 'act' is DRAN, whereas the Athenian word is PRATTĒIN.)

So much for the different subdivisions of imitation, and what they amount to.

Origins of Poetry: (a) Imi-tation CHAPTER 4. There seem to be two causes that gave rise to poetry in general, and they are natural. The impulse to imitate is inherent in man from his childhood; he is distinguished among the animals by being the most imitative of them, and he takes the first steps of his education by imitating. Every one's enjoyment of imitation is also inborn. What happens with works of art demonstrates this: though a thing itself is disagreeable to look at, we enjoy contemplating the most accurate representations of it—for instance, figures of the most despicable animals, or of human corpses. The reason for this lies in another fact: learning is a great pleasure, not only to philosophers but likewise to every one else, however limited his gift for it may be. He enjoys looking at these representations, because in the act of studying them he is learning—identifying the

object by an inference (for instance, recognizing who is
the original of a portrait); since, if he happens not to have
already seen the object depicted, it will not be the imitation
as such that is giving him pleasure, but the finish of the
5 workmanship, or the colouring, or some such other cause.

And just as imitation is natural to us, so also are music   (b) *Music*
and rhythm (metres, clearly, are constituent parts of   *and*
rhythms). Thus, from spontaneous beginnings, mankind   *Rhythm*
developed poetry by a series of mostly minute changes out
10 of these improvisations.

But a temperamental difference of character caused   *Develop-*
poetry to break sharply into two. The more serious   *ment*
writers imitated illustrious doings, involving illustrious
persons; the lighter-minded imitated those of low people,
15 at first in the form of flytings, while the others were
writing hymns and encomiums. We cannot tell of any
such light poem by any one before Homer, though it is
likely that there were many who wrote them, but beginning
with Homer we can: his *Margītēs*, for instance, and similar
20 works. (It was here that the iambic metre came into use,
in virtue of its appropriateness for the purpose; that is
how the metre got its present name, because it was the
name of the lampoons in which they attacked each other.
So it came about that some of the early poets wrote in
25 heroic verse and others in iambics.) And just as Homer was
the great exemplar of high poetry, being the only poet
who not only wrote nobly but also made dramatic[1]
imitations, so too he was the first to adumbrate the outlines of comedy by making his drama not vituperative but
30 ludicrous; in fact the relationship between the *Margites* and
our comedies is analogous to that between the *Iliad* and
Odyssey and our tragedies. But as soon as tragedy and
comedy had become available, those whose natural tempera-

[1] Probably explained by 51.13–17.

21

ments impelled them towards one or the other kind of poetry wrote comedies instead of lampoons, and tragedies instead of epics, because comedy and tragedy were grander and esteemed more highly. To examine whether or no the organic evolution of tragedy is now complete, and to settle 5 that question both absolutely and in relation to the stage, does not belong to our present discussion.

Going back to the improvisations in which it at first consisted (and so did comedy—tragedy began with the leaders of the dithyramb, and comedy with the leaders of 10 the phallic performances which still survive as customary practices in many of our cities), it grew up little by little as its character became clear and its form was developed. So after many transformations, tragedy settled down when its nature was formed. Aeschylus first increased the 15 number of actors from one to two, reduced the chorus part, and put the chief weight on the speeches; Sophocles introduced three actors and scene-painting. As to its amplitude: it acquired its serious character at a late stage, when it outgrew slight fables and grotesque language in the 20 process of transformation from satyr-drama; and at the same time the metre changed from trochaic tetrameters to iambics. At first they used the tetrameter, because their poetry was satyr-poetry and more akin to the dance; but when it began to be spoken, the very nature of the thing 25 found its right metre, for the iambic is the best adapted of all metres to speech. For a demonstration of this: we use iambics most often in conversation with one another, but hexameters seldom, and by way of a departure from normal intonation.—(Also, division of the play into acts.)[1] 30 Lastly, we may pass over all the superficial graces of tragedy; for it would no doubt be a long business to go through their whole history in detail.

[1] See Note A, p. 62.

CHAPTER 5. Comedy is, as I have said, an imitation of *Defini-* lower types; though it does not include the full range *tions:* of badness, nevertheless to be ridiculous is a kind of 1. *Comedy* deformity. The causes of laughter are errors and disgraces
5 not accompanied by pain or injury; the comic mask, for instance, is deformed and distorted, but not painfully so. We know something of the stages through which tragedy passed and the men to whom they were due, but there are no early records of comedy, because it was not
10 highly valued. It was a long time before comic dramas were licensed by the magistrate; the earlier comedies were produced by amateurs. Comedy had already acquired certain outlines by the time of the earliest comic poets whose names are known. Who added masks or prologues
15 or extra actors, and other such matters, we have no means of knowing. The fable-structure first came from Sicily (Epicharmus and Phormis); at Athens, Cratcs was the first to drop the lampoon form and make unified stories, that is to say fables.

20 Epic poetry coincides with tragedy *in so far as it is an 2. *Epic* imitation, in metrical speech,*[1] of high people; but they differ in that the epic has the same metre throughout and is in narrative form. They also differ in length, because tragedy tends as far as possible to keep within a single
25 day and night or thereabouts, whereas the epic has no time-limit; though at first tragic poets followed the epic in this respect. As for their elements, some are the same and some are peculiar to tragedy. Accordingly, any one who can tell a tragedy of high value from a poor one can do the
30 same for an epic; for tragedy has everything that the epic has, but the epic has not everything that there is in tragedy.

[1] Or, according to Bywater: 'to this extent, that of being an imitation....in a grand kind of verse'. But Aristotle has just said that the predominant metre of tragedy is not grand (p. 22, ll. 23–30).

3.*Tragedy* CHAPTER 6. Of the art that imitates in hexameters, and of comedy, we will speak later; let us now discuss tragedy, having first picked up from what has been said the definition of its essence that has so far emerged. Tragedy, then, is an imitation of an action of high importance, complete 5 and of some amplitude; in language enhanced by distinct and varying beauties; acted not narrated; by means of pity and fear effecting its purgation of these emotions. By the beauties enhancing the language I mean rhythm and melody; by 'distinct and varying' I mean that some are 10 produced by metre alone, and others at another time by melody.

Elements   Now since the imitating is done by actors, it would follow of necessity that one element in a tragedy must be the *Mise en scène*. Others are Melody and Language, for 15 these are the media in which the imitating is done. By Language I mean the component parts of the verse,[1] whereas Melody has an entirely sensuous effect. Again, since the object imitated is an action, and doings are done by persons, whose individuality will be determined by their 20 Character and their Thought[2] (for these are the factors we have in mind when we define the quality of their doings), it follows that there are two natural causes of these doings, Thought and Character; and these causes determine the good or ill fortune of every one. But the Fable is the 25 imitation of the action; and by the Fable I mean the whole structure of the incidents. By Character I mean the factor that enables us to define the particular quality of the people involved in the doings; and Thought is shown in everything they say when they are demonstrating a fact or 30 disclosing an opinion. There are therefore necessarily six

[1] Bywater translates: 'the composition of the verses'. The sense is not clear. But see p. 26, ll. 24-6, and p. 55, ll. 12-14.
[2] See Note B, p. 66, and Note D, p. 76.

24

elements in every tragedy, which give it its quality; and they are the Fable, Character, Language, Thought, the *Mise en scène*, and Melody. Two of these are the media in which the imitating is done, one is the manner of imitation, and three are its objects; there is no other element besides these. Numerous poets have turned these essential components to account; all of them are always present—the *Mise en scène*, Character, the Fable, Language, Melody, and Thought.

10   The chief of these is the plotting of the incidents; for tragedy is an imitation not of men but of doings, life, happiness;[1] unhappiness is located in doings, and our end is a certain kind of doing, not a personal quality; it is their characters that give men their quality, but their doings
15 that make them happy or the opposite. So it is not the purpose of the actors to imitate character, but they include character as a factor in the doings. Thus it is the incidents (that is to say the Fable) that are the end for which tragedy exists; and the end is more important than anything else.
20 Also, without an action there could not be a tragedy, but without Character there could. (In fact, the tragedies of most of the moderns are non-moral, and there are many non-moral poets of all periods; this also applies to the paintings of Zeuxis, if he is compared with Polygnōtus, for whereas
25 Polygnotus is a good portrayer of character the painting of Zeuxis leaves it out.) Again, if any one strings together moral speeches with the language and thought well worked out, he will be doing what is the business of tragedy; but it will be done much better by a tragedy that handles these
30 elements more weakly, but has a fable with the incidents connected by a plot. Further, the chief means by which tragedy moves us, Irony of events and Disclosure,[2] are

---

[1] See Note D, pp. 79–80.
[2] See Chapter 11, pp. 31–2, and Note D, pp. 81–2.

elements in the Fable. A pointer in the same direction is that beginners in the art of poetry are able to get the language and characterization right before they can plot their incidents, and so were almost all the earliest poets.

So the source and as it were soul of tragedy is the Fable; and Character comes next. For, to instance a parallel from the art of painting, the most beautiful colours splashed on anyhow would not be as pleasing as a recognizable picture in black and white. Tragedy is an imitation of an action, and it is chiefly for this reason that it imitates the persons involved.

Third comes Thought: that is, the ability to say what circumstances allow and what is appropriate to them. It is the part played by social morality[1] and rhetoric in making the dialogue: the old poets made their characters talk like men of the world, whereas our contemporaries make them talk like public speakers. Character is what shows a man's disposition—the kind of things he chooses or rejects when his choice is not obvious. Accordingly those speeches where the speaker shows no preferences or aversions whatever are non-moral. Thought, on the other hand, is shown in demonstrating a matter of fact or disclosing a significant opinion.

Fourth comes the Language [*of the speeches*].[2] By Language I mean, as has already been said, the expressive use of words. It has the same force in verse as in prose.

Of the remaining elements, Melody is the chief of the enhancing beauties. The *Mise en scène* can excite emotion,

[1] Aristotle's word is 'Politics'; but the Greek word covered a wider field than its modern homonym. 'Men of the world' corresponds to 'Politics'; 'public speakers', to rhetoric.

[2] The Greek is doubtful, and the phrase is unnecessary; I believe it is an interpolation. Bywater's rendering ('Fourth among the literary elements is the Diction') is based on an emendation, and is equally doubtful.

but it is the crudest element and least akin to the art of
poetry; for the force of tragedy exists even without stage
and actors; besides, the fitting out of a *Mise en scène* belongs
more to the wardrobe-master's art than to the poet's.

5 CHAPTER 7. So much for analysis. Now let us discuss   *Fable*
in what sort of way the incidents should be plotted, since
that is the first and chief consideration in tragedy. Our
data are that tragedy is an imitation of a whole and complete
action of some amplitude (a thing can be whole and yet
10 quite lacking in amplitude). Now a whole is that which
has a beginning, a middle, and an end. A beginning is
that which does not itself necessarily follow anything else,
but which leads naturally to another event or development;
an end is the opposite, that which itself naturally (either of
15 necessity or most commonly) follows something else, but
nothing else comes after it; and a middle is that which itself
follows something else and is followed by another thing.
So, well plotted fables must not begin or end casually, but
must follow the pattern here described.

20   But, besides this, a picture, or any other composite   *Ampli-*
object, if it is to be beautiful, must not only have its parts   *tude*
properly arranged, but be of an appropriate size; for
beauty depends on size and structure. Accordingly, a
minute picture cannot be beautiful (for when our vision
25 has almost lost its sense of time it becomes confused); nor
can an immense one (for we cannot take it all in together,
and so our vision loses its unity and wholeness)—imagine
a picture a thousand miles long! So, just as there is a proper
size for bodies and pictures (a size that can be kept in view),
30 there is also a proper amplitude for fables (what can be kept
well in one's mind). The length of the performance on the
stage has nothing to do with art; if a hundred tragedies
had to be produced, the length of the production would be

settled by the clock, as the story goes that another kind of performance once was.[1] But as to amplitude, the invariable rule dictated by the nature of the action is the fuller the more beautiful so long as the outline remains clear; and for a simple rule of size, the number of happenings that will make a chain of probability (or necessity) to change a given situation from misfortune to good fortune or from good fortune to misfortune is the minimum.

Unity CHAPTER 8. Unity in a fable does not mean, as some think, that it has one man for its subject. To any one man many things happen—an infinite number—and some of them do not make any sort of unity; and in the same way one man has many doings which cannot be made into a unit of action. It seems, therefore, that all the poets who have composed *Heracleïds*, *Theseïds*, and suchlike, made a mistake; people think that because Hēracles was one man it follows that his fable has unity. Homer, as always, is an exception; he seems to have seen this admirably well, either by art or by nature. In writing his *Odyssey* he did not include everything that happened to Odysseus (for instance, his wound on Parnassus, or his pretence of madness at the mobilization, since there was no necessity or probability that either of these events should have led to the other); but he confined the plot of the *Odyssey* to an action that has the kind of unity I mean, and he did the same with the *Iliad*. Accordingly, just as in the other imitative arts the object of each imitation is a unit, so, since the fable is an imitation of an action, that action must be a complete unit, and the events of which it is made up must be so plotted that if any of these elements is moved or removed the whole is altered and upset. For when a thing can be

---

[1] This is obscure. Margoliouth explains it as an allusion to the prostitute Klepsydra in a lost comedy.

included or not included without making any noticeable difference, that thing is no part of the whole.

CHAPTER 9. From what has been said it is also clear *Prob-* that it is not the poet's business to tell what has happened, *ability*
5 but the kind of things that would happen—what is possible according to probability or necessity. The difference between the historian and the poet is not the difference between writing in verse or prose; the work of Herodotus could be put into verse, and it would be just as much a
10 history in verse as it is in prose. The difference is that the one tells what has happened, and the other the kind of things that would happen. It follows therefore that poetry is more philosophical and of higher value than history; for poetry universalises[1] more, whereas history particularises.
15 The universal occurs when a man says or does what is characteristic of his temperament, probably or necessarily, in the circumstances (this is the point of the descriptive proper names in poetry); what Alcibiades did or what happened to him is an aggregation of particulars. In
20 comedy this has now become clear. They first plot the fable on a base of probabilities, and then find imaginary names for the people—unlike the lampooners, whose work was an aggregation of personalities. But in tragedy they keep to real people. This is because possibility depends on
25 conviction; if a thing has not happened we are not yet convinced that it is possible, but if it has happened it is clearly possible, for it would not have happened if it were impossible. Even tragedies, however, sometimes have all their persons fictitious except for one or two known names;
30 and sometimes they have not a single known name, as in the *Anthos* of Agathon, in which both the events and the names are equally fictitious, without in the least reducing

[1] See Note C, pp. 72-3.

29

the delight it gives. It is not, therefore, requisite at all costs to keep to the traditional fables from which our tragedies draw their subject-matter. It would be absurd to insist on that, since even the known legends are known only to a few, and yet the delight is shared by every one. 5

From all this, then, it is clear that the poet must be a maker of fables rather than of verses, in that he is a poet by virtue of his imitation and what he imitates is doings. And even if he happens to make a poem out of real events, he will not *ipso facto* cease to be a poet; for there is nothing 10 to prevent some things that have happened from being in accordance with probability as well as possibility, in virtue of his poetic handling of them.[1]

Simple Of simple fables, those whose action is episodic are the
fables worst. By an episodic fable I mean one in which scene 15 follows scene without probability or necessity. Such tragedies are written by bad poets of their own accord, and by good ones because of the actors—they write for theatrical effect and expand the fable more than it can bear, so that they are often forced to dislocate the sequence of events. 20 True, the action imitated must contain incidents that evoke fear and pity, besides being a complete action; but this effect is accentuated when these incidents occur logically as well as unexpectedly, which will be more sensational than if they happen arbitrarily, by chance. Even when 25 events are accidental the sensation is greater if they appear to have a purpose, as when the statue of Mitys at Argos killed the man who had caused his death, by falling on him at a public entertainment. Such things appear not to have happened blindly. Inevitably, therefore, plots of this sort 30 are finer.

[1] Or 'and it is in that aspect of them that he is their poet' (Bywater).

CHAPTER 10. Some fables are simple, others complex: for the obvious reason that the original actions imitated by the fables are the one or the other. By a simple action I mean one that leads to the catastrophe in the way we
5 have laid down, directly and singly, without Irony of events or Disclosure.

An action is complex when the catastrophe involves *Complex* Disclosure, or Irony, or both. But these complications *fables* should develop out of the very structure of the fable, so
10 that they fit what has gone before, either necessarily or probably. To happen after something is by no means the same as to happen because of it.

CHAPTER 11. Irony[1] is a reversal in the course of events, *Irony of* of the kind specified, and, as I say, in accordance with *Events*
15 probability or necessity. Thus in the *Oedipus* the arrival of the messenger, which was expected to cheer Oedipus up by releasing him from his fear about his mother, did the opposite by showing him who he was; and in the *Lynceus* ⟨Abas⟩, who was awaiting sentence of death, was acquitted,
20 whereas his prosecutor Dănaüs was killed, and all this arose out of what had happened previously.

A Disclosure, as the term indicates, is a change from *Dis-* ignorance to knowledge; if the people are marked out for *closure* good fortune it leads to affection, if for misfortune, to
25 enmity. Disclosure produces its finest effect when it is connected with Irony, as the disclosure in the *Oedipus* is. There are indeed other sorts of Disclosure: the process I have described can even apply to inanimate objects of no significance, and mistakes about what a man has done or
30 not done can be cleared up. But the sort I have specified is

[1] The Greek word here is PERIPETEIA. It has been sufficiently adopted to appear in some English dictionaries. Bywater anglicizes it into 'Peripety'. See Note D, pp. 81–2.

more a part of the fable and of the action than any other sort; for this coupling of Irony and Disclosure will carry with it pity or fear, which we have assumed to be the nature of the doings tragedy imitates; and further, such doings will constitute good or ill fortune. Assuming then that it is a disclosure of the identity of persons, it may be of one person only, to the other, when the former knows who the latter is; or sometimes both have to be disclosed— for instance, the sending of the letter led Orestes to the discovery of Iphigeneia, and there had to be another dis- closure to make him known to her.

Crisis of *feeling* This then is the subject-matter of two elements in the Fable, Irony and Disclosure. A third element is the Crisis of feeling. Irony and Disclosure have been defined; the Crisis of feeling is a harmful or painful experience, such as deaths in public, violent pain, physical injuries, and everything of that sort.

Sections *of a Greek* *tragedy* CHAPTER 12. We have mentioned previously the generic elements that should be employed in writing a tragedy. Now as to the separate sections into which it is divided: they are Prologue, Epeisŏdion, Exodos, and Chorus (divided into Parŏdos and Stăsĭmon)—these are common to all tragedies; Songs by actors, and Kommos—these are optional. The Prologue is the whole section of a tragedy before the choric Parodos; an Epeisodion is a complete section of a tragedy between complete choric songs; the Exodos is the whole section of a tragedy after which there is no song by the chorus. In the choric part, the Parodos is the first passage of words by the whole chorus; a Stasimon is a song of the chorus not in anapaests or trochees; a Kommos is a lamentation in which both chorus and actors take part. We have mentioned previously the elements that should be employed in writing a tragedy;

the separate sections into which it is divided have now been given.[1]

CHAPTER 13. Following the proper order, the next subject to discuss after this would be: What one should aim at and beware of in plotting fables; that is to say, What will produce the tragic effect. Since, then, tragedy, to be at its finest, requires a complex, not a simple, structure, and its structure should also imitate fearful and pitiful events (for that is the peculiarity of this sort of imitation), it is clear: first, that decent people must not be shown passing from good fortune to misfortune (for that is not fearful or pitiful but disgusting); again, vicious people must not be shown passing from misfortune to good fortune (for that is the most untragic situation possible—it has none of the requisites, it is neither humane, nor pitiful, nor fearful); nor again should an utterly evil man fall from good fortune into misfortune (for though a plot of that kind would be humane, it would not induce pity or fear—pity is induced by undeserved misfortune, and fear by the misfortunes of normal people, so that this situation will be neither pitiful nor fearful). So we are left with the man between these extremes: that is to say, the kind of man who neither is distinguished for excellence and virtue, nor comes to grief on account of baseness and vice, but on account of some error; a man of great reputation and prosperity, like Oedipus and Thyestes and conspicuous people of such families as theirs. So, to be well formed, a fable must be single rather than (as some say) double—there must be no change from misfortune to good fortune, but only the opposite, from good fortune to misfortune; the cause must not be vice,

The Tragic Pattern

---

[1] See Note A, p. 64. This chapter is of no importance except to the historian of Greek tragedy, and not much to him. I have therefore not translated the technical terms.

but a great error; and the man must be either of the type specified or better, rather than worse. This is borne out by the practice of poets; at first they picked a fable at random and made an inventory of its contents, but now the finest tragedies are plotted, and concern a few families—for example, the tragedies about Alcmeon, Oedipus, Orestes, Mĕlĕāger, Thyestes, Tēlĕphus, and any others whose lives were attended by terrible experiences or doings.

This is the plot that will produce the technically finest tragedy. Those critics are therefore wrong who censure Euripides on this very ground—because he does this in his tragedies, and many of them end in misfortune; for it is, as I have said, the right thing to do. This is clearly demonstrated on the stage in the competitions, where such plays, if they succeed, are the most tragic, and Euripides, even if he is inefficient in every other respect, still shows himself the most tragic of our poets. The next best plot, which is said by some people to be the best, is the tragedy with a double plot, like the *Odyssey*, ending in one way for the better people and in the opposite way for the worse. But it is the weakness of theatrical performances that gives priority to this kind; when poets write what the audience would like to happen, they are in leading strings. This is not the pleasure proper to tragedy, but rather to comedy, where the greatest enemies in the fable, say Orestes and Aegisthus, make friends and go off at the end, and nobody is killed by anybody.

The Mise en scène CHAPTER 14. The pity and fear can be brought about by the *Mise en scène*; but they can also come from the mere plotting of the incidents, which is preferable, and better poetry. For, without seeing anything, the fable ought to have been so plotted that if one heard the bare facts, the chain of circumstances would make one shudder and pity.

34

That would happen to any one who heard the fable of the
Oedipus. To produce this effect by the *Mise en scène* is less
artistic and puts one at the mercy of the technician; and
those who use it not to frighten but merely to startle have
5 lost touch with tragedy altogether. We should not try to
get all sorts of pleasure from tragedy, but the particular
tragic pleasure. And clearly, since this pleasure coming
from pity and fear has to be produced by imitation, it is by
his handling of the incidents that the poet must create it.

10 Let us, then, take next the kind of circumstances that *The*
seem terrible or lamentable. Now, doings of that kind *Tragic*
must be between friends, or enemies, or neither. If an *Mode:*
enemy injures an enemy, there is no pity either beforehand *Pity and*
or at the time, except on account of the bare fact; nor is *Fear*
15 there if they are neutral; but when sufferings are engendered
among the affections—for example, if murder is done or
planned, or some similar outrage is committed, by brother
on brother, or son on father, or mother on son, or son on
mother—that is the thing to aim at.

20 Though it is not permissible to ruin the traditional
fables—I mean, such as the killing of Clytemnestra by
Orestes, or Erïphÿle by Alcmeon—the poet should use
his own invention to refine on what has been handed down
to him. Let me explain more clearly what I mean by
25 'refine'. The action may take place, as the old poets used
to make it, with the knowledge and understanding of the
participants; this was how Euripides made Medea kill her
children. Or they may do it, but in ignorance of the horror
of the deed, and then afterwards discover the tie of
30 affection, like the Oedipus of Sophocles; his act was outside
the play, but there are examples where it is inside the
tragedy itself—Alcmeon in the play by Astÿdămas, or
Tēlĕgŏnus in *The Wounded Odysseus*. Besides these, there is
a third possibility: when a man is about to do some fatal

act in ignorance, but is enlightened before he does it. These are the only poss'ble alternatives. One must either act or not act, and either know or not know. Of these alternatives, to know, and to be about to act, and then not to act, is thoroughly bad—it is disgusting without being tragic, for there is no emotional crisis; accordingly poets only rarely create such situations, as in the *Antigone*, when Haemon fails to kill Creon. Next in order is to act; and if the deed is done in ignorance and its nature is disclosed afterwards, so much the better—there is no bad taste in it, and the revelation is overpowering. But the last is best; I mean, like Mĕrŏpe in the *Cresphontes*, intending to kill her son, but recognizing him and not killing him; and the brother and sister in the *Iphigeneia*; and in the *Helle*, the son recognizing his mother just as he was going to betray her.—This is the reason for what was mentioned earlier: that the subject-matter of our tragedies is drawn from a few families. In their search for matter they discovered this recipe in the fables, not by cunning but by luck. So they are driven to have recourse to those families where such emotional crises have occurred.

That is all that need be said about the plotting of the incidents, and what the fables should be like.[1]

Character CHAPTER 15. In Character there are four things to aim at. First and foremost, that it should be good of its kind: a speech or action will be moral if (as I have said) it shows a preference, and the morality will be good if the preference is good of its kind. This is possible in every class. There are good women and good slaves; yet the former class is no doubt inferior, and the latter altogether low.—Secondly, that it should be appropriate: for instance, *any one can have a brave character, but there are kinds of courage, as

[1] See Note A, p. 64.

well as kinds of sagacity, that may be inappropriate to a
woman.*[1]—Thirdly, that it should be lifelike; this is distinct
from making the character good and appropriate as defined
above.—And fourthly, that it should be consistent; even
5 if the person who is the original of the imitation is inconsistent, and inconsistency is the basis of his character, it
is none the less necessary to make him consistently inconsistent. An example of an unnecessarily low character is
Menelaus in the *Orestes*; of the unseemly and inappropriate,
10 the lament of Odysseus in the *Scylla*, and the speech of
Mĕlănippe; of the inconsistent, Iphigeneia at Aulis—her
character as a suppliant is quite unlike her later self.

And in the characterization, as in the plotting of the
incidents, the aim should always be either necessity or
15 probability: so that they say or do such things as it is
necessary or probable that they would, being what they
are; and that for this to follow that is either necessary or
probable. (Thus it is clear that the untying[2] of the fable
should follow on the circumstances of the fable itself, and
20 not be done *ex machina*, as it is in the *Medea*, or in Book 2
of the *Iliad*. But the *deus ex machina* should be used for
matters outside the drama—either things that happened
before and that man could not know, or future events that
need to be announced prophetically; for we allow the gods
25 to see everything. As for extravagant incidents, there should
be none in the story, or if there are they should be kept
outside the tragedy, as is the one in the *Oedipus* of
Sophocles.)[3]

Since tragedy is an imitation of people above the normal,
30 we must be like good portrait-painters, who follow the

---

[1] Or, according to Bywater: 'The Character before us may be, say,
manly; but it is not appropriate in a female Character to be manly, or
clever.' See Note D, p. 78.
[2] See Chapter 18 (41.18–27).   [3] See 54.19–22.

original model closely, but refine on it; in the same way the poet, in imitating people whose character is choleric or phlegmatic, and so forth, must keep them as they are and at the same time make them attractive. *So Homer made Achilles noble, as well as a pattern of obstinacy.*[1]   5

Look out for these points; and also for aesthetic effects mixed up with though not relevant to poetry, for they too can often lead to failure. But enough has been said about them in the published works.

Kinds of Disclo-sure CHAPTER 16. What Disclosure is has been explained   10 above; the different species of Disclosure are as follows. First, the most inartistic, and usually a makeshift, Disclosure by visible clues. They may be birth-marks, like 'the spear-head that the Earth-born bear', or the stars in the *Thyestes* of Carcinus; or they may be acquired, either   15 physical marks such as scars, or accessories like necklaces and the disclosure in the *Tyro* by the skiff. But even with these clues there are degrees of badness, according to the way they are used; for instance, Odysseus was disclosed by his scar in one way to the nurse and in another way to the   20 herdsmen. Used deliberately as passports they are more inartistic—indeed this applies to any kind of disclosure used for that purpose—whereas those that come from an irony in the events (like the one in Book 19 of the *Odyssey*) are better.   25

Next come those that are made by the poet and are on that account inartistic. Thus in the *Iphigeneia*, Orestes himself disclosed who he was: Iphigeneia was disclosed by her letter, but the poet tells her (through the mouth of Orestes) what he wants her to know, instead of making the   30 fable do it. This is nearly as faulty as the former kind, for

[1] Or, according to Bywater: 'as Agathon and Homer have represented Achilles.'

Orestes might just as well have handed something to her. Or again, the 'tale told by the loom' in the *Tēreūs* of Sophocles.

Thirdly, through a memory, by the awakening of a sense of something familiar: like the disclosure in the *Cyprians* of
5 Dĭcaeogĕnes, when ⟨Teucer⟩ burst into tears at the sight of the picture; or in Book 8 of the *Odyssey*, when the memories revived by hearing the harper made ⟨Odysseus⟩ weep. So they disclosed who they were.

Fourthly, by logic; as in the *Chŏēphŏri* ('A man like me
10 has come; there is no man like me but Orestes; therefore he has come'). And the disclosure suggested by Polyīdus the sophist for the *Iphigeneia*: it is probable that Orestes would have drawn the parallel between the sacrificing of his sister and the accident that he himself was being
15 sacrificed. And in the *Tȳdeūs* of Theodectes, the speech about coming to find his son and being lost himself. And the one in the *Phīneīdae*: when they saw the place they argued that it was their fate—they were fated to die at that place, because they had been exposed there in infancy.
20 There is a composite form of this species, built on a fallacy in the mind of the audience; as in the *Odysseus disguised as a Messenger*. *That ⟨Odysseus⟩ and no one else can string the bow is put into the poem by the poet, and this is the premise ⟨from which we start⟩, especially since
25 ⟨Odysseus⟩ said he would string the bow though he had not seen it; but the fallacy is that the poet makes us think ⟨Odysseus⟩ is going to disclose himself in that way, and then makes him do so in another way.*[1]

But of all disclosures the best are those that arise out of
30 the story itself and cause astonishment by probable events; as in the *Oedipus* of Sophocles, and the *Iphigeneia*—it is

---

[1] The manuscript followed by Bywater has a lacuna of several words, which deprives this example of its point. See the note on this passage on p. 86.

probable that she would want to send a letter. These are the only ones without prefabricated clues, or necklaces. The next best are the logical kind.

Imagi- CHAPTER 17. When you are putting together your
nation fables and working out the composition in words, you 5
should as far as possible set the play before your eyes;
those who see in this way, as though they were present at
the performance, will find the right thing in its most vivid
form, and make the fewest unconscious blunders. This is
borne out by the trouble Carcinus got into; if the spectator 10
did not actually see Amphiăraüs appearing out of the
temple he would not notice it, but when it was staged the
audience took it amiss and damned the play. You should
even as far as possible act the parts as you compose the
speeches; for the best way of making a man's emotions 15
convincing is to take his very nature to yourself—the
manifestations of stormy or angry feelings are most lifelike in a man who is himself in a storm or rage. Poetry
therefore goes with genius or madness; for the former is
responsive, and the latter subject to delusions. 20

Reduc- Whether the story is an old one or whether you are
tion and yourself making it up, you should first reduce it to a signi-
Inter- ficant and unified outline, and afterwards expand and inter-
polation polate your scheme. By viewing a story in unified outline,
I mean this kind of thing (from the *Iphigeneia*). A girl was 25
sacrificed; vanished from the sight of her sacrificers; was
deposited in another country, where there was a custom of
sacrificing strangers to the goddess; became the priestess
of the goddess; some time afterwards the brother of the
priestess turned up there (that he was sent there by an 30
oracle for a reason, and his purpose in going, are no part
of the fable); having arrived he was arrested; was about to
be sacrificed; revealed himself—either as Euripides made

it happen, or, in the probable way Polyidus worked out,
by saying that not only his sister but he too had to be
sacrificed; hence their escape. This done, you should now
interpolate, with the individuality of the people as your
5 foundation; and take care that your interpolations are
correctly particularized—for example, by making the
capture of Orestes depend on his madness, and using the
purification to bring about their escape.

Now in plays these scenes are concise; but epic poetry
10 owes its length to them. The story of the *Odyssey* is *⟨not⟩*
long: a man is abroad for many years; Poseidon has his
eye on him; he is alone; his home too is in a bad way, for
suitors are using up his property and plotting against his
son; he suffers shipwreck; gets home; discloses who he
15 is; makes an attack in person; gets safely off and destroys
his enemies. This is the substance; everything else is interpolation.

CHAPTER 18. Every tragedy consists in the tying and *Tying*
untying of a knot. What is outside the play, and usually *and*
20 also some of the incidents inside it, are the tying; and the *Untying*
rest is the untying. By the tying, I mean from the beginning
up to the point immediately before the change to good
fortune or misfortune; and by the untying, from the
beginning of the change to the end. Thus in the *Lynceus*
25 of Theodectes, the tying is what happened before the play,
together with the arrest of the boy; *and ⟨the untying⟩ of
these events again is from the capital indictment to the end.*[1]

There are four kinds of tragedy, for that is the number *The*
of elements we specified: Complex tragedy, which consists *Kinds of*
30 entirely of an ironical plot with Disclosure; Emotional *Tragedy*

[1] See the note on p. 86. After this sentence, Bywater inserts the
passage at the end of the next paragraph (p. 42, ll. 10–14), transferring
it from its place in the manuscripts.

tragedy, like the *Ajax* and *Ixīon* plays; Moral tragedy, like the *Women of Phthia* and the *Pēlēus*; and fourthly *Spectacular* tragedy,[1] like the *Phorcides* and the *Prometheus* and all the stories located in Hades. But try to develop all the elements of tragedy if you can, or at least as many as 5 possible of the most important, especially considering the unfair fault-finding poets suffer from nowadays; as there have already been poets who have done well with each of the elements separately, every one is expected to outdo all their specialities single-handed. Yet to discriminate justly 10 between tragedies one should concentrate on the fable: that is, the tangling and untying of the knot. Many writers tangle it well and then untie it badly; but it is necessary always to master both.[2]

Miscel- And you should remember what has been said many 15
laneous times, and not try to make an epic compilation into a
Injunc- tragedy—by epic I here mean multifabular. For example,
tions suppose one were to try and work the whole fable of the
Iliad into a tragedy. In the epic, because of its length, the
parts can be properly developed, but to do so in a play 20
often turns out to be an error of judgement. For instance,
all the poets who have written whole *Falls of Troy* instead
of taking parts of the story as Euripides did, or whole
Niōbes instead of following the example of Aeschylus,
either fail completely or do badly on the stage. Indeed, 25
even Agathon had a play damned for this alone. But both
in the use of Irony, and in simple stories, *he is*[3] remark-

[1] The name of the fourth kind of tragedy is lost in a hopeless corruption of the Greek text. For want of anything better I accept Bywater's conjecture. But cf. p. 52, ll. 13–15.

[2] These two sentences need not be moved. Aristotle is contrasting unfair fault-finding with the right way of judging plays.

[3] In the manuscripts the verb is in the plural (Bywater: 'the poets I mean show wonderful skill in aiming at the kind of effect they desire'). I follow an old conjecture, accepted by Butcher.

42

ably successful in what they aim at, which is to be tragic
and satisfy human feeling; as when he shows us a clever
but wicked man (like Sīsyphus) outwitted, or a brave
unscrupulous man put down. That kind of situation is also
5 probable; as Agathon says, we must expect the unexpected
often to happen.[1]

Treat the chorus as though it were one of the actors; it
should be an organic part of the play and reinforce it,
not as it is in Euripides, but as in Sophocles. In their
10 successors the songs belong *⟨no⟩* more to the fable than
to that of any other tragedy. This has led to the insertion
of borrowed lyrics, an innovation for which Agathon was
responsible. Yet what difference is there between inserting
a borrowed lyric and sticking in a speech or a whole act
15 from another play?

CHAPTER 19. So much for the other elements; it *Thought*
remains to discuss Language and Thought. As for Thought,
I have nothing to add to what is said about it in my
Rhetoric, since it is more germane to that subject. Thought
20 controls all the effects that have to be produced by
language: including proof—refutation—the manipulation
of feelings such as pity, fear, anger, and so forth—as well
as aggrandizement and depreciation. Clearly also you
require Thought on the same lines for the incidents,
25 whenever you need to make them pathetic or terrible, or
larger than life or probable; with this much difference, that
you have to make the point clear without stating it, whereas
in the language the effects are produced by a speaker in so
many words. Indeed, what would be the use of the dialogue
30 *if the pleasure were obvious*[2] without words?

---

[1] See Note C, p. 74.
[2] Or, according to Bywater: 'if things appeared in the required
light'.

Language About Language: one approach to it is Syntax. Knowledge of this concerns the performer's art, and those trained
in the scientific side of style: for instance, the distinction
between command and entreaty, exposition and threat,
question and answer, and so forth. A man's knowledge or   5
ignorance of these matters is irrelevant to the serious
censure of his poetry. When Protagŏras censures 'Sing,
Goddess, of the wrath', because Homer, intending to
entreat, is giving a command—for the imperative, with or
without a negative, denotes a command—how could any   10
one accept that as a fault? Let us then pass over this branch
of theory as relevant not to poetry but to another art.

Units of CHAPTER 20. Quantitatively, the units of Language are:
Language Speech-sounds, Syllables, Ligatures, Nouns, Verbs,†[1]
Inflexions, Statements.   15
A Speech-sound is an indivisible sound; but not all
indivisible sounds, only those of which intelligible words
are in fact composed—beasts make indivisible sounds, but
I do not include these. Speech-sounds are divided into
Vowels, Semi-vowels, and Mutes. A Vowel is an audible   20
sound with the mouth open; a Semi-vowel is an audible
sound with a contact in the mouth (like S or R); a Mute is
made with a contact in the mouth, has no sound by itself,
but combined with an audible sound it becomes audible
(for instance hard G, or D). Speech-sounds differ according   25
to the way the mouth is shaped, the place where they are
articulated, whether they are aspirated or voiced or
breathed, long or variable or short, acute or neutral or
grave. The enumeration and study of speech-sounds is
a branch of phonetics.   30

[1] † (line 14). I follow Butcher and Rostagni in deleting a word here
('the Article' in Bywater's translation), and also a passage on the next
page.

44

A Syllable is a meaningless sound consisting of a consonant and a vowel or semi-vowel: for example GRA is a syllable, and so is GR without the A. But the study of the different kinds of syllable also belongs to phonetics.

5 A Ligature is: either a meaningless sound that can be combined with other sounds in a unit of sense but cannot make them into a complete unit of sense (the group of sounds can come at either end of the unit of sense or in the middle, but it is a mistake to put the ligature itself at
10 the beginning of the sentence)—these ligatures are the particles; or a meaningless sound that can make a single unit of sense out of a number of such units. †[1]

A Noun is a composite sound with meaning, independent of time, its component parts being separately meaningless;
15 for in compound nouns we do not attach a separate meaning to the parts—in the name Theodore the -*dore* no longer stands for anything.

A Verb is a composite sound with meaning, to which a time-connotation is added; its component parts, like
20 those of the Noun, do not mean anything separately. The word *man* or *white* does not tell you the time when, but the word *walks* denotes in addition the present time, and the word *walked* denotes past time.

Inflexions occur in nouns and verbs; they denote
25 relationship (*his* or *him*, and so forth), or number (*man* or *men*); or they may be made by intonation, as in question or command—*walk?* and *walk!* are verb-inflexions of this kind.

A Statement is a composite sound with meaning, some

---

[1] † (line 12). I omit here a paragraph rendered by Bywater: 'An Article is a non-significant sound marking the beginning, end, or dividing-point of a Speech, its natural place being either at the extremities or in the middle.' This does not make sense, and no amount of emendation can make any sense of the Greek. I think it is spurious. See previous footnote.

of whose parts have a separate meaning of their own. It is not true that every statement must contain a noun and a verb—there can be statements without a verb, like the definition of 'man'; but it must always have a part with a separate meaning, as *Cleon* has in the statement 'Cleon is 5 walking'. A statement is a unit, but it can be so in two different ways: either because it means one thing, or because it consists of several statements joined together by ligatures. The *Iliad* is a unit by means of ligature; the definition of 'man', because it has a single meaning. 10

Kinds of CHAPTER 21. Names are classed as single, by which
Name I mean that the parts of which they are composed are meaningless, as in *earth*; or double (those composed of one part with meaning and one without, the compound as a whole having a meaning; and those composed of parts 15 both of which have meanings). Names can also be triple, or quadruple, or multiple, (like most of the grandiose proper names such as Hermocaïcoxanthus).

Names divide into: Standard words, Loan-words, Metaphors, and Fancy words (new-coined, or expanded, 20 or abbreviated, or otherwise altered).

By a Standard word I mean one that we all use; by a Loan-word, one in general use elsewhere. So it is clear that a word may be both a standard word and a loan-word, but not in the same country; for example the standard 25 word for 'spear' in Cyprus (sĭgÝnon) is a loan-word here.

Metaphor is the attribution of a name belonging to something else: either from the genus to the species, or from the species to the genus, or from species to species, 30 or by analogy. 'Here lies my ship' is from genus to species, for to be moored is a kind of lying. 'Ten thousand brave deeds has Odysseus done' is from species to genus,

for ten thousand is many, and so it has come to be used in place of 'many'. An example of metaphor from species to species is the pair of expressions 'Draining the life-blood with the metal' and 'Cutting with unyielding metal', where
5 'draining' and 'cutting' have been used as interchangeable terms, for both are kinds of severance. By analogy I mean when one thing is in the same relation to another as a third thing is to a fourth, and the speaker uses the fourth for the second or the second for the fourth; and sometimes people
10 add to the metaphor the object to which its homologue is related. For example, the cup of Dionysus corresponds to the shield of Āres; so the cup will be called the shield of Dionysus, and the shield the cup of Ares. Again, old age is to life as the evening is to the day; so the evening will be
15 called the dying day, or old age, as Empedocles called it, the evening of life, or the sunset of life. Even when some of the homologues have no standard name, the same figure of speech can be used: for instance, scattering the grain is called sowing, whereas for the sun's scattering of
20 its beams there is no specific word; but this act is to the sun's rays as sowing is to the grain, hence the expression 'sowing his heavenly flame'. This sort of metaphor can also be used in another way: having called the object by its new name, you then negate one of its attributes. Thus the shield
25 might be called, not the cup of Ares, but 'the cup that none drink wine from'.

A new-coined word is one not previously used at all in any community but supplied by the poet (for there seem to be some such words): like 'branchets' for horns, and
30 'litanist' for priest.

An expanded word is one that has a vowel longer than in the proper pronunciation, or an extra syllable; and its opposite is a word from which something has been left out. Examples of expansion are PŎLĔŎS for PŎLĔŌS, and

PĒLĒĬĂDĒO for PĒLEĪDOŪ; of abbreviation, KRĪ ⟨for KRĪTHĒ⟩, DŌ ⟨for DŌMĂ⟩, and OPS ⟨for OPSIS⟩ at the end of the line ⟨in Empedocles⟩. Alteration occurs when part of the word is retained and part is new-coined, as in DEXĪTĔRON for DEXĪON (*Iliad*, Book 5, l. 393). 5

Names in the strict sense[1] are either masculine, or feminine, or intermediate. The masculines are those that end in ν, ρ, *⟨ς⟩*, and the two consonants compounded with ς (ψ and ξ); the feminines, those that end in certain vowels—the vowels that are always long (η and ω), and 10 one of the vowels that can be long (α). It happens, therefore, that the number of letters in which masculine and feminine nouns end is equal; for ψ and ξ are variants *⟨of ς⟩*. No noun ends in a mute or in a vowel that is always short. Only three end in ι (MĔLĬ, KOMMĬ, and PĔPĔRĬ). 15 Five end in υ. The intermediates end in this kind of letter, and in ν, *⟨ρ⟩*, and ς.

Poetic CHAPTER 22. The virtue of language is to be clear
Diction without being low. Language formed of standard words is
clearest, but it is low: for example, the poetry of Cleŏphon 20
or Sthĕnĕlus. Out-of-the-way usages give dignity and
transform the common speech; by 'out-of-the-way' I mean
loan-words, metaphors, extended words, and all departures
from the standard. But if any one uses these kinds of
language exclusively, the result will be either a puzzle, 25
or gibberish: nothing but metaphor would be a puzzle,
and nothing but loan-words would be gibberish. The
idea of a puzzle is to piece together into sense elements
which as they stand are nonsense, and it is impossible
to do this with a sentence composed of ordinary terms, 30

---

[1] I.e. *nouns*. It is curious and interesting that Aristotle considered this paragraph relevant to poetry (cf. p. 44, ll. 11–12). But blunders in accidence matter more in poetry than syntactical freedoms.

but with one composed of metaphors it is possible: for
instance,
> 'With fire a man I once beheld
> Bronze upon another weld',[1]

5 and all the quips of that kind. (Gibberish of loan-words.)[2]

These devices should therefore only be used to flavour
the language; then the loan-words, and metaphors, and
fancy words, and the other kinds I have mentioned, will
prevent commonness and lowness, and the standard words
10 will make the sense clear. But the element that contributes
most to clearness of language without commonness is
expanded, curtailed, or altered words; for being unfamiliar
because of its variation from standard speech, this will
prevent commonness, and at the same time clearness will
15 be preserved by the partial familiarity of the words.
Therefore, to condemn this manner of speech and ridicule
the writers who use it is mistaken censure: like the elder
Euclid's remark that it is easy to write poetry if you are
given permission to lengthen syllables as much as you like,
20 and his lines satirizing the practice by the style they are
written in,
> 'Epícharés walkéd to Márathón'

and
> '*Buy hís hellébore fór lovérs' complaints.*'[3]

25 Certainly, to parade your use of this device is ridiculous;
but all the elements of language alike have their due
proportion, and to use metaphors or loan-words, or any

---

[1] The solution of this feeble conundrum is 'A cupping-bowl'.

[2] I.e. 'Insert here an instance of gibberish made up of foreign
words.' See Note A, p. 62.

[3] The Greek is corrupt and obscure. For purposes of translation
I accept Margoliouth's suggestion that this line is part of an advertise-
ment. The point of Euclid's parodies is two-fold: the style is prosaic,
and to make the lines into verse you have to lengthen some of the
syllables improperly.

other kind of language, outrageously or with the deliberate
intention of being funny would produce the same effect.
But an appropriate use of it gives great distinction to verse,
as you may observe in epic poetry if you put in the ordinary
words. With loan-words and metaphors too, and the other 5
forms of language, any one who substituted the standard
words would see that what I say is true. For instance,
there is an iambic line written by Aeschylus and Euripides,
the same except for one word; it is by custom a standard
word and is replaced by a loan-word, and whereas the 10
old line seems commonplace, the new one seems fine.
Aeschylus in his *Philoctētes* wrote

    'The cancer eating up the flesh of my foot',

and Euripides changed 'eating up' to 'gorging on'. Or if
the line 15

    'I that am dwarfish, naught, and of ill favour'

were altered (by substituting standard words) into

    'I that am small, an invalid, and ugly'.

Or
    'Setting a menial stool and lowly table' 20

to
    'Setting a kitchen stool and little table',

or 'the roaring sea-shore' to 'the noisy sea-shore'. Or
again Ariphrădes ridiculed tragic dramatists for using
expressions that no one would use in conversation, like 25
'from the house afar' (instead of 'far from the house'), and
'thine', and 'her I wedded', and 'Achilles round' (instead
of 'around Achilles'), and so on; because they are not in
the standard form all such expressions make for un-
commonness of diction, but he ignored this. 30

Now though all the devices I have mentioned, if they
are properly used, give distinction—double words as well
as loan-words—far the greatest distinction is to be metaphorical; for it is the only one that demands originality and

is a sign of genius; for to make good metaphors is to perceive similarity.

Double words suit the dithyramb best, loan-words suit the hexameter, and metaphors the iambic. And whereas all of them may be used in hexameter verse, in iambic verse (since it imitates conversation as closely as possible) only those words are suitable which would be used in a speech: and they are the standard word, the metaphor, and fancy word.

This is all I need to say about tragedy, or imitation by means of actors.

CHAPTER 23. Now for the poetry that imitates in *Epic* narrative verse. Clearly, its fables should be put together dramatically, as in tragedies; concerning a single whole and complete action with a beginning, middle, and end, in order that it may give its own individual pleasure like a single whole picture. They should not be composed like histories, whose writers have to present not a single action but a single period and everything that happened in it to one or more persons, with a purely accidental relationship of one event to the others. For just as the battle of Salamis and the Carthaginian action in Sicily happened at the same time without any bearing towards the same end to link them together, so in chronological sequences one thing sometimes happens after another without leading to any single end. But most of our poets are mere chroniclers. As I have already said, Homer stands out miraculously above the others, and one can see it here too. Although the war had a beginning and an end, he did not attempt to get the whole of it into his poem; he would have thought it too long to be kept in view, or (even if its length were manageable) over-complicated by its variety. As it is, he selected one item and made use of many others as incidental

interpolations: the catalogue of ships, for example, as well as
other interpolations with which he embroiders his poetry.
The others write either a biography of a single man, or
a chronicle of a period, or if they take a single action they
treat it piecemeal: like the author of the *Cypria* or of the
Little Iliad. Accordingly an *Iliad* or an *Odyssey* makes a
single tragedy or not more than two, but a *Cypria* makes
several; and in the *Little Iliad* there are more than eight—
*The Armour of Achilles, Philoctetes, Neoptolemus, Eurypÿlus,
The Beggar Spy, The Spartan Women, The Sack of Troy,* and
The Sailing of the Fleet; not to mention *Sinon* and *The Trojan
Women*.

Com- CHAPTER 24.   Again, epic poetry inevitably has the
parison same kinds as there are in tragedy—either Simple, or
with Complex, or Moral, or Emotional; and the same elements,
Tragedy except Melody and *Mise en scène*—for it needs Irony of
events, and Disclosure, and Crises of feeling; and the
thoughts and language must also be well formed.   Homer
not only was the first to make use of all these but also used
them satisfactorily.   Thus of his two poems one, the *Iliad*,
is simple and emotional, whereas the other, the *Odyssey*,
is complex (Disclosure is constantly occurring) and moral.
Not only so, but they excel all other poems in language and
thought.

But epic poetry differs in the size of the plot, and in
metre.   As for size, the definition I have given is sufficient:
we must be able to survey it from beginning to end.   That
would be so if the plots were smaller in bulk than those
of the old epics but about the equal of all the tragedies
produced at one hearing.[1]   Epic poetry has a property that
tends to increase its amplitude considerably.   In tragedy it is

[1] Obscure; but it must mean either 'on one day' or 'during one
competition'.   Probably the former.

not possible to imitate several parts of a story as happening at the same time, but only the part played by the actors on the stage; in the epic, because it is a narrative, many simultaneous transactions can be depicted, by which, if
5 they are related to one another, the weight of the poem will be increased. So that it has the merit of richness, diverting the audience by the interpolation of dissimilar scenes; for monotony soon surfeits, and this can make a tragedy fail.

As for metre, the heroic metre has established itself by
10 experience. If any one wrote narrative imitation in any other metre, or in several metres, it would be obviously improper; for heroic verse is more deliberate and weightier than any other, which enables it to absorb loan-words and metaphors better, and makes narrative imitation the most
15 uncommon of the arts. The iambic and the trochaic tetrameter are mobile, the latter being akin to the dance and the former to drama. And it would be an even worse blunder to mix metres, in the manner of Chaerēmon. Accordingly, no one has ever written a poem with an extended plot in
20 any metre other than the heroic; as I have said, the very nature of a thing teaches us to choose what is appropriate to it.

Many as Homer's merits are, he deserves especial praise for knowing what part to play himself in his poems. The
25 poet must say very little in his own person; for so far as he does that, he ceases to be an imitator. Now whereas all other poets are perpetually coming on the stage themselves, and use imitation seldom and scantily, Homer, after a short prologue, at once brings in a man or a woman or
30 some other character—no one of them non-moral, but all with character.

Sensational matter must be included in tragedies, but extravagance (which is the chief factor in producing a sensation) is easier to introduce in epic poetry, because we do not see the actor. The pursuit of Hector would be obviously absurd on the stage—⟨Achilles⟩ shaking his head, and the army standing still instead of joining in the chase; but occurring in the epic it is not noticed. And the sensational gives pleasure; for instance, every one spices 5 news with it, as a bait.

Homer more than any one else has taught other writers the correct way of telling an untrue story: that is, by the use of an unnoticed fallacy. When one fact or happening is always accompanied by another fact or happening, people 10 think that the second is always accompanied by the first; but that is not true. So, if the first is false, and there is some concomitant of it that is true, the concomitant must be introduced into the story; for if we know that the second fact is true, our mind infers falsely that the first also is so. 15 (Example from Book 19 of the *Odyssey*.)[1]

Probable impossibilities are to be preferred to unconvincing possibilities. The plot of a story should not be made up of extravagances. Preferably there should be nothing extravagant in it; but if there is, it should be 20 outside the tale, like the ignorance of how Laïus came to be killed in the *Oedipus*, and not in the drama, like the report of the Pỹthian games in the *Electra*, or that a man should have come from Tĕgĕa to Mỹsia without speaking, as in the *Mysians*. So it is ridiculous to say that the fable 25 would be ruined; no plot of that sort should ever be made in the first instance. But if, having done so, one could clearly have done it in a more acceptable way, that is a blunder indeed—even in the *Odyssey* it is clear that the extravagances about the landing ⟨on Ithaca⟩ would have been intolerable 30 if they had been written by a bad poet. As it is, the poet makes his blunder delightful, blinding us to it by his general excellence. But the language should only be

[1] See Note A, p. 62, and note on p. 86.

54

highly-wrought in the neutral passages, where there is no
Character or Thought; for Morality, and Thought also,
are obscured by over-brilliant writing.

CHAPTER 25. *Critical exercises and how to get them right.* *Practical*
5 The different kinds of exercise, and the quality of each, may *Criticism*
be made clear by the following theoretical considerations:

Since the poet is an imitator, just like a painter or any
other maker of images, he must necessarily always be
imitating one of the following (three in number): either
10 things as they were or are, or things as they are said or
thought to be, or things as they ought to be.

These imitations are expressed in language, including
loan-words and metaphors—and there are many other
modifications of language, which we allow poets to use.

15 Further, the standard of rightness is not the same in
poetry as it is in social morality, or indeed in any other art.
But even in poetry there are two kinds of fault, one
essential and the other incidental. *Inability to imitate
according to one's concept is a fault of the poetry itself*;[1]
20 but if an inaccuracy in the concept—like depicting a horse
with both his off-legs thrown forward—has introduced into
the poem a scientific error (say in physiology or some other
science), or any other impossibilities whatever, it is not an
essential fault.

25 So you must keep your eye on these principles in doing
exercises that involve a censure on the poet.

First, criticisms touching the essentials of the art.
'Impossibilities have been put into the poem.' That is
a fault. But it is all right provided the art attains its end,

[1] Or, according to Bywater's conjecture: 'If the poet meant to
describe the thing correctly, and failed through lack of power of
expression, his art itself is at fault.' I follow Margoliouth's conjecture
which agrees better with p. 56, ll. 8–9.

which I have specified—provided, that is, they enable it to
make the incident, or another incident, more impressive.
Example: the pursuit of Hector. If, however, the end
could also have been attained more or less[1] by conforming
to the science of the object involved, it is not all right; 5
for if possible there should be no errors anywhere at all.
Again, is the error in the art itself, or is it only in an
incidental matter? For instance, it is less serious not to
know that a hind has no horns than to paint her indistinctly.

Next, if the criticism is 'That is not true'. Perhaps the 10
answer is 'No, but it ought to be'; as Sophocles said
'I depict man as he ought to be, whereas Euripides depicts
him as he is'. If that will not do, there is tradition: as in
the stories about gods, which are no doubt what Xĕnŏ-
phănes says they are, neither better than the truth, nor 15
true; still, they pass for true. And in some instances
perhaps the answer is not 'It is better than the truth', but
'It used to be true': as in the statement in *Iliad* 10. 152-3
'their spears were planted upright on the butt-end'; that
was then the custom, as it is to this day among the Illyrians. 20

In making moral judgements of a speech or action, you
must consider not only the statement or act itself, to see
whether it is good or bad, but also *who* is doing or saying
it *to whom, on what occasion, in what way*, and *for what reason*
(e.g. whether it is to produce a greater good, or prevent 25
a greater evil).

Other difficulties must be solved by examining the
language. For instance:

Foreign usage. The word OURĒAS in *Iliad* 1. 50 no doubt
means 'sentries', not 'mules'. Or the description of Dolon 30

---

[1] Or, according to Bywater: 'as well or better'; this involves an
emendation of the Greek. But it seems likely from l. 6 that Aristotle
thought some sacrifice of effectiveness justified for the sake of scientific
accuracy.

in *Iliad* 10. 316, which means not that his body was deformed but that his face was ugly, 'well-figured' being the Cretan expression for handsome. Or *Iliad* 9. 203, which means 'mix the wine quicker', not 'stronger' (as though for topers).

5   Or *Metaphor*. For example: 'The others, gods and men, slept the whole night long', though at the same time he says 'Indeed, whenever he turned towards the plain of Troy, ⟨he marvelled at⟩ the noise of flutes and pipes'; where 'all' has been used metaphorically for 'many', since *all*
10 is a species of *many*. So also 'alone' in *Iliad* 18. 489 is metaphorical; ⟨there are others, but⟩ the best known representative is made to stand for the whole group.

Or *Phonetics*: e.g. Hippias the Thasian's proposals, ⟨to move the accent on⟩ DĬDŎMEN (*Iliad* 2.15), and ⟨aspirate⟩
15 OU (*Iliad* 23. 328).

Or the *Grouping of words*: e.g. in Empedocles, 'Soon mortal grew what had before known immortality, and things pure before mixed'.[1]

Or a *Verbal Ambiguity*: e.g. in *Iliad* 10. 252–3, ⟨which
20 means⟩ 'a full two-thirds of the night is past', ⟨not 'more than two-thirds'⟩; the word PLEO can have either meaning.

Or an *Extension of customary usage*. Wine diluted with water is called 'wine': so, ⟨in *Iliad* 21. 592,⟩ the poetic expression 'the greave of newly-wrought tin'. Again,
25 blacksmiths are called 'coppersmiths': so Ganymede is said ⟨in *Iliad* 20. 234⟩ to 'pour wine to Zeus', though they do not drink wine.[2] But this usage should very likely be explained as metaphorical.

Whenever a word seems to contradict the sense, you
30 must investigate all the meanings it could have in the

---

[1] The ambiguity is whether 'before' goes with 'pure' or 'mixed'.
[2] In the first example, 'tin' is put instead of *bronze* (the part for the whole); in the second, 'wine' instead of *nectar* (the human drink for the divine). Cf. p. 47, ll. 2–6.

context: e.g. in *Iliad* 20. 272, in how many senses it could be said to have been 'stopped by that one'. Is this the meaning, or is that? This way of making conjectures is diametrically opposite to the one described by Glaucon: 'they jump at an assumption without thinking, and, having themselves laid down the law against the poet, draw conclusions from it; they ascribe to him a statement invented by themselves, and then censure him for it if it is inconsistent with their own opinions'. That is what has happened in the controversy over Icarius. They fancy he was a Lacedemonian, and therefore that it was a blunder not to make Telemachus meet him when he went to Lacedaemon. But what the Cephallenians say may be the truth of the matter: they assert that Odysseus married one of their countrywomen, and that ⟨her father's name⟩ was Icadius, not Icarius. So the criticism is probably based on a mistake.

SUMMARY. Impossibilities. To be accounted for by (*a*) poetic licence, (*b*) improvement, (*c*) opinion.

(*a*) Poetic licence. A convincing impossibility is preferable to what is unconvincing even though it is possible.

(*b*) 'The people are like portraits by Zeuxis':[1] so much the better—one should improve on the model.

(*c*) Extravagances to be accounted for by popular tradition. Also sometimes by denying that it is extravagant; for we must expect the unexpected to happen sometimes.

Verbal inconsistencies. Study them as one studies logical fallacies. His subject must be the same, and be in the same context, and have the same significance, if he ⟨is to be blamed for contradicting⟩ what he has himself said, or what every sensible man assumes.

[1] Cf. 19. 4. It appears that Zeuxis resembled Polygnotus in idealizing his portraits, though he differed from him by 'leaving character out' (p. 25, ll. 24-6).

But the censure of extravagances, or of lack of dignity
⟨in the characters⟩, is valid when they are not inevitable and
no use is made of them: like the improbable arrival of
Aegeūs in Euripides, or the undignified behaviour of
5 Menelaus in the *Orestes*.

Censure, then, derives from five kinds of criticism: that
it is impossible, or extravagant, or immoral, or inconsistent, or technically incorrect. And you must find the
answers to it by keeping your eye on the factors I have
10 mentioned, of which there are twelve.[1]

CHAPTER 26. You may wonder whether epic or tragic *Superi-*
imitation is the better. If the less popular art is the better, *ority of*
and if by less popular you mean 'appealing to a higher-class *tragedy*
public', it is all too clear that an art that imitates everything[2]
15 is popular. As though we cannot perceive anything unless
it is actually thrust upon us, they go through a multitude
of movements: like low-class flute-players, who sway about
if they have to imitate discus-throwing, and drag the
conductor down if they are playing a *Scylla*. Now that is
20 what tragedy is like. The older actors had just such an
opinion of those who came after them; Mynniscus called
Callipīdes 'Jackanapes' because of his over-acting, and
much the same was thought of Pindărus. But as the later
actors were to the earlier, so the whole dramatic art is to the
25 epic. It is said that the epic appeals to a fit audience who
do not need posturings, whereas tragedy appeals to a low-
class audience. So if it is a popular art, it must clearly be
worse.

[1] Various unconvincing attempts have been made to add up the
items enumerated at the beginning of the chapter (p. 55, ll. 7-24).
It does not matter greatly.
[2] Or, according to Bywater: 'an art addressing any and every one';
but this involves an emendation, and is less in accord with the next
sentence.

First: this attack does not concern the poet's art, but the performer's; for rhapsodes too can overdo their gestures (for instance Sōsistrătus), and so can professional singers, as Mnāsithĕŭs of Opus did. Again, not all physical movement is to be banned, or we should have to ban dancing; but only unmannerly movements, which is another thing Callipides was censured for, and some of our present actors too—that they imitate women who are not respectable. And again, tragedy can do her specific work without any physical movement, in the same way as epic poetry does; from a reading of the text the whole meaning is apparent. So if she is otherwise superior, that is not one of her necessary properties.

Secondly then: since Tragedy has everything the Epic has (she can even use the epic metre), and in addition the considerable elements of Music and the *Mise en scène*, by which our pleasures are set in most vivid motion; again, she is vivid enough in the mere reading, and has the added vividness of stage performance; again, she achieves the end of the imitation in a shorter length, and what is more compact gives greater pleasure than what is spun out for a long time, as you will realize if you imagine the *Oedipus* of Sophocles re-written in as many lines as there are in the *Iliad*; again, the imitation by epic poets has less unity (by way of evidence, any one such imitation goes to make several tragedies; if they write one with a single fable, it either is told rapidly and seems abrupt, or has to be watered down in order to reach the proper length; but I mean one combining several actions, like the *Iliad* and the *Odyssey*, which contain many such sections, each of some amplitude; and yet the Homeric poems are plotted as well as they could be, and the action they imitate is as unified as possible)—

If, then, tragedy is superior in all these ways, and also in fulfilling her artistic function (for the mere giving of

pleasure is not enough, they must give the kind of pleasure
I have specified), it would seem clear that she is better than
epic poetry, because she achieves her end better.

That is all I have to say about tragedy and epic poetry, *Finis*
both in general, and how their different species and
elements are to be distinguished, and what are the causes
of their success or failure, and about different kinds of
critical censure and the answers to them.

NOTES

A. INCOMPLETENESS OF THE *POETICS*

THAT this treatise is incomplete is obvious from internal evidence; and there is an old tradition that it originally consisted of two books (see Introduction, p. 1). The incompleteness of the *Poetics* shows itself both in the style and in the subject-matter.

I. STYLE

Some of Aristotle's works were written for the general public (the 'published works' referred to at the end of Chapter 15, 38.9), but almost all those that have survived, including the *Poetics*, are lectures written for the instruction of his own pupils. The style of the *Poetics*, as Gilbert Murray says,[1] 'suggests the MS. of an experienced lecturer, full of jottings and adscripts, with occasional phrases written carefully out, but never revised as a whole for the general reader'. I have put the most obvious of these adscripts in round brackets, for instance 'Also, division of the play into acts' (22.30), and 'Example from Book 19 of the *Odyssey*' (54.16). But even apart from this the book seems, as Professor Murray says, to be unrevised and unfinished. The whole of Chapter 25 is in skeleton form, and at least one note elsewhere (49.5) appears to indicate a gap waiting to be filled. As for the style in general, Professor Murray somewhat exaggerates its scrappiness, though he justly describes it as luminous and vivid. It is a highly individual style, of its kind excellent, and most of the treatise will go into good enough English without much amplification.

[1] Preface to Bywater's translation, 1920.

2. SUBJECT-MATTER

Aristotle's treatment of poetry strikes most modern readers at first sight as inadequate; but this is because of a change in the use of the word 'poetry', and adds nothing to the evidence that the *Poetics* is incomplete. The strongest evidence is provided by some of Aristotle's own statements. At the beginning of Chapter 6 he promises to speak later of comedy; and in a passage in the *Politics* in which he applies his theory of purgation to music, he says he will give a clearer account of that theory in the *Poetics*. Our text does not carry out either of these undertakings. Its last sentence ('That is all I have to say *about tragedy and epic poetry . . .*'), together with these two unfulfilled promises, led Bywater to assert that in the Second Book of the *Poetics* Aristotle dealt at length with comedy, and with his theory of purgation. There is also a curious manuscript of the tenth century[1] which looks like the summary of an analysis of comedy on lines parallel to Aristotle's analysis of tragedy.

But there is little reason to suppose that much of importance has been lost. After his treatment of tragedy, Aristotle only needed two chapters for the epic; would he have needed more than five or six for comedy? We should like to know for certain what emotions he thought comedy purges;[2] we should like to know more of what he had to say about Character and Fable in comedy, and perhaps a little more about comic Language than the hint at the beginning of Chapter 22. But even as it is we have

[1] Known as the *Codex Coislinianus*. See Lane Cooper, *An Aristotelian Theory of Comedy* (1924), which makes the most of this evidence. But the document does not mention Aristotle's name. I agree with Bywater, who judges it to be a 'sorry fabrication'.

[2] According to the *Cod. Coislinianus* they are *pleasure* (? i.e. sensual appetite) and *laughter*.

enough material to reconstruct the outlines of his theory of comedy.

As for purgation, it is mentioned only once in this treatise, in the final clause of the definition of tragedy in Chapter 6 ('by means of pity and fear effecting its purgation of these emotions'). Aristotle professes to be putting the definition together 'from what has been said'; so it looks as though something about purgation had dropped out of the early part of the treatise. But it is equally possible, and perhaps more probable, that he intended to insert some-where in the early section an explanation of purging similar to his explanation of imitating at the beginning of Chapter 4, and never got it done. Fortunately the gap is not as serious as it might have been, since the passage in the *Politics* makes the meaning of purgation clear. It means the provision of an outlet for burdensome and disagreeable emotions.

Apart from gaps in the subject-matter, Aristotle would surely have rearranged some of the chapters if he had finished the work. Chapter 12 comes in awkwardly; it would be more in place at the end of the section on tragedy, before the last sentence of Chapter 22. Worse still, at the end of Chapter 14 he closes the section on plot, only to revert to it in the very next chapter (37.18–28) and then to devote three more whole chapters to it (Chapters 16–18). But these last defects are common in Aristotle's works; lectures are never 'finished'.

B. THE DEFINITION OF POETRY

IN spite of its opening words ('Let us talk of the art of poetry as a whole'), the *Poetics* nowhere gives a clear definition of the extent and limits of poetry. Disaster usually attends such definitions, and we may therefore applaud Aristotle's caution—or congratulate him on his oversight. The only safe answer to the question 'What did Aristotle mean by poetry?' is 'The activity, and the products, about which he wrote in the *Poetics*'. And, taken all together, it is a treatise on fiction,[1] rather than on what the word 'poetry' has stood for to the common reader for the last hundred and fifty years. So I have entitled my translation 'Aristotle on the Art of Fiction'.

But there is an obvious objection: the *Poetics* is incomplete. If, as some maintain, we have only about half of the whole work, we cannot be sure that in the other half Aristotle did not greatly extend the range of poetry. Therefore it is necessary to search the text we possess for any passages in which he defines the essence or marks out the frontiers of poetry. Such passages turn out to be neither numerous nor conclusive.

I. IMITATION

In Chapter 1 he gives a list of four of the main kinds of Greek poetry—epic, tragedy, comedy, and dithyramb—and classes them, together with instrumental music and the plastic arts, as 'imitations'. But this does not explicitly lay it down that *all* poetry is imitation. There is a statement more to our purpose in Chapter 9: 'From all this, then, it is clear that the poet must be a maker of fables rather than of verses, in that *he is a poet by virtue of his imitation*, and what he imitates is doings' (30.6–8). This is confirmed by his earlier complaint, in Chapter 1, that people class writers 'not as poets in virtue of the act of imitating' but according to the metre in which they write; Empedocles 'should be called a scientist rather than a poet' (18.7–14). The phrase

[1] In *Timber*, summing up the Aristotelian view of poetry, Ben Jonson defined the poet as 'a maker or a feigner' and his art as 'an art of imitation or feigning'. 'Feigning', of course, means 'fiction'. Cf. Margoliouth, p. 44.

I have italicized fixes Aristotle's outside limit for poetry; but it is not of course a complete definition, for though nothing is poetry that is not imitation, there are other species of imitation that are not poetry.

According to Aristotle, all the arts are further defined by *what* they imitate, and by the *medium* in which they do so. Of plastic artists he says simply that they 'imitate many things' (17.13); of dancers, that they 'imitate characters and experiences and doings' (17.21–2). In the important sentence I have quoted from Chapter 9, he says that what 'the poet' imitates is doings; but by this time he is thoroughly embarked on his analysis of tragedy, and 'the poet' here probably means the tragic poet. This is confirmed by other statements specifically limited to tragedy: for instance, in Chapter 6, it is because tragedy is concerned with happiness and unhappiness that 'it is not the purpose of the actors to imitate character, but they include character as a factor in the doings' (25.15–17). This argument does not apply to comedy; nor does a similar passage in Chapter 14 (35.7–9). We cannot therefore be sure how Aristotle defined the subject-matter of poetry as a whole. But one important limitation is suggested in Chapter 19, where he says that Thought is more germane to rhetoric than to poetry. 'Thought', in Aristotle's system, is the personal part of a man's inner life: his reasonings ('What is the truth of the matter?'); his sentiments; his mental images (43.19–23). Thought is an *ingredient* in poetry, because it is a part of personality (24.20–1) and doings imply persons. But it is not the *object* of the imitation; that is to say, the poet's specific work is not expression. His work is to give a picture of the outside world, including Thought only so far as it is a (minor) factor in that objective world. This is the main difference between Aristotle's theory of poetry and most modern theories.

'Imitation' is not of course limited to the copying of particular objects in such a way as to cause illusions, as at Madame Tussaud's. Aristotle does not exclude that sense of the word; indeed he seems to regard it as the simplest and most obvious sense (20.25–9). But the poetic imitator does not merely depict appearances; he recreates the very life that he is contemplating (40.15–16). Nor need that life be 'real'; the situations and the persons can be altogether imaginary. In its full sense, imitation means producing as accurately as possible the effect that a situation, or an experience, or a person, would produce in its true natural form, without the intrusion of extraneous or irrelevant accidents: which, of course, seldom happens in real life. In that sense Aristotle's theory can be applied to every kind of poetry, even the least dramatic of lyrics; and so applied it appears to me almost identical with Wordsworth's doctrine of 'emotion recollected in tranquillity'.

Ross[1] goes so far as to say that when in the *Politics* Aristotle ranks music as the most imitative of the arts he 'can only mean that it is the most expressive, that which most successfully embodies emotion'. No doubt that is so; but it does not follow that even the musician is seeking to give an image of *his own* emotional state, that he is aiming at *self*-expression. He is aiming to exert the force of an experience that he has observed or imagined; that is the implication of Aristotle's first principle for all the 'fine' arts.

In fact Aristotle confines himself in the *Poetics* to narrative and dramatic poetry. I do not think it likely that purely lyrical poetry formed part of the supposed Second Book. The Greeks seem to have regarded personal poetry as a kind of rhetoric; even 'Longinus', the author of the treatise 'On the Sublime' (which was written some five

[1] Chapter IX, p. 278.

hundred years after the *Poetics*), applies roughly the same criteria to Sappho's famous ode as to the speeches of Demosthenes.

(See also Introduction, pp. 9–10.)

2. MEDIUM

Aristotle nowhere defines the medium of poetry as a whole; but he implicitly excludes kinds of imitation that do not use language at all. On the other hand he explicitly includes music, rhythm (and therefore dancing), and even scenery, costume, and the actor's art, among the media of poetry. A dramatic poem is not for him merely the words, but the whole performance.

It is not certain whether Aristotle considered metre a necessity of poetry. The question is obscured by a textual crux in Chapter 1 (**17**.22–5). The trouble about this highly elliptical note is that Aristotle's use of the word 'epic' has the sense of 'in hexameter verse' (see **18**.5–7 and **24**.1); to say that such poems are either in prose or verse is therefore nonsense. Accordingly all the modern editors except Margoliouth reconstruct the Greek text into a quite different statement based on the Arabic version; this is the reading Bywater follows in his translation (quoted in my footnote 2 on page 17).

But Aristotle is struggling with a gap in the critical vocabulary of his time. It lacked a term for what he calls in the next chapter 'the art that uses prose, or verse without music', the class that includes both the Homeric epics and such works of imaginative fiction as Plato's *Symposium*. He disapproves of the Greek habit of classifying poems according to their metre (**18**.5–14); it was one of his principles that metre does not modify the effect of language (**26**.26); and he more than once insists that the verse-form in no way

even helps to make poetry of a work that does not satisfy
the essential requirements (cf. 29.8–10). The manuscript
reading represents a note rather than a finished sentence,
and as a note it makes sense. It was natural to proceed from
lyric to dancing and so to epic poetry; natural to point out
that for any one 'imitating' by language alone there is a
choice between verse and prose; and characteristic of
Aristotle to add that in fact heroic poetry had up to his time
always been written in hexameters. His objection to the
term 'epic poetry' was not inflexible: later in the *Poetics* he
gradually reconciles himself to it, by way of two intermediate periphrases (24.1 and 51.12–13).

In short, he seems to have held that the verse-form was
not essential for poetry, but that it was justified by experience. On the one hand, the poet is not primarily a
maker of verses; on the other hand 'the very nature of
a thing teaches us to choose what is appropriate to it'
(53.20–22).

C. THE FABLE

(See also Introduction, pp. 10–11.)

1. The Greek word is MYTHOS. Most modern versions
translate it 'plot'; but I prefer the closer rendering 'fable',
which was used by our older critics in the sixteenth and
seventeenth centuries. Aristotle has a separate word for
plot; and the word MYTHOS stands for something less
abstract than a mere plan or design. It is true that he defines
it in Chapter 6, from the poet's point of view, as 'the
whole structure (SYNTHESIS) of the incidents' (24.26–7);
but by this he means exactly the same as by his earlier and
better definition in Chapter 5 ('unified stories, that is to

say fables': **23**.18–19). Moreover the subject-matter of the Homeric epic, and of almost all Greek tragedy, is legend-ary; the significance of these poems lies in the twist the poet gives to the familiar myth.[1]

(In Aristotle's two main classifications of Fables there is a confusion of terms. At the beginning of Chapter 13 he distinguishes between 'simple' and 'complex' fables (**33**.7), and he has already clearly explained this distinction in Chapter 10. But later in Chapter 13, he speaks of 'single' and 'double' fables (**33**.27–8): single fables ending in general disaster, whereas double fables (as in our melo-dramas) end in the triumph of the good characters and the ruin of the bad. Aristotle uses the same word for 'simple' and 'single'; I have ventured to use different words.)

2. DOINGS, ACTION; EXPERIENCE, FEELING

By defining a Fable as 'the imitation of the action' (**24**.25–6) Aristotle gives his notion of the relationship between poetry and real life. An Action is a unit of life (**25**.11), either actual or invented; a Fable is what the poet makes of that Action.

Under the general heading of Action two Greek words are involved: PRAXIS (what a man does) and PĂTHOS (what happens to him). But PRAXIS is also used in a wide sense, to include PATHOS, and cover the whole of a man's life at any given time; and this is the sense it usually has in the *Poetics*. Whenever possible I have therefore translated it 'doing', which suggests a wider range of events than 'action'—when we say a man is 'doing well', we include his condition and circumstances as well as his activities. But Aristotle commonly uses the word for a *unit* of

[1] See again Gilbert Murray, loc. cit. p. 8. The whole paragraph, and indeed the whole Preface, is full of valuable suggestions.

happenings involving several people; and for this there is no suitable English word except 'an action'. The word I translate 'incident' (PRAGMA) belongs to the same etymological group; it means a separate item in an Action.

PATHOS (Experience) is also Aristotle's word for 'emotion', which the Greeks generally regarded as an experience rather than a voluntary activity; it is applied to pity and fear in Chapter 6 (24.7–8). At the end of Chapter 11 Aristotle uses it in a special sense, defined as 'a harmful or painful experience' (32.15). The word bears this sense in the story of the life of Christ, where it is translated 'Passion'. I render it 'Crisis of Feeling'.

3. THE WHOLE, UNITY, THE UNIVERSAL

Aristotle lays it down in his definition of tragedy that the action imitated is a 'complete' action (24.5), and in Chapter 7 he returns to that requirement ('tragedy is an imitation of a whole and complete action': 27.8–9). In Chapter 8 he uses the word 'one' ('a unit of action': 28.14). 'Universality' is one of his most characteristic concepts. In logic he defines it as 'what can be predicated of more than one'; but neither this definition, nor the English word, explains the weight carried by this concept in Aristotle's theory of poetry.

In Chapter 17 he speaks of universalising a story (40.22–3), and gives two examples: which show that he means eliminating everything that does not contribute to the general effect of the story, and making one event lead up to another. The process is *unification*, and the result a *significant* plot. The word is also applied to a story in Chapter 5 (23.18), where it appears to be used in the same sense. Again, when in Chapter 6 he says that Thought is shown in disclosing a universal opinion (26.22–3), he surely does not mean a 'general' opinion (a platitude, or a sententious observation), but an opinion that contributes to the total effect of the play; it is meant to exclude irrelevant or merely picturesque elements in the dialogue. Here it is best translated 'significant'.

In Chapter 9 Aristotle contrasts history unfavourably with poetry because history enumerates particulars, whereas poetry tends to 'universalise' (29.13–19). Again he gives an example: which is not a definition, and should be read in conjunction with the parallel passage in Chapter 23, where Aristotle uses the words 'whole' and 'complete' but does not use the word 'universal'. In Bywater's translation, the statement runs: 'poetry is something more philosophic and of graver import than history, since its statements are of the nature rather of universals, whereas those of history are singulars. By a universal statement I mean one as to what such or such a kind of man will probably or necessarily say or do....' From this one might conclude that for Aristotle the value of poetry consists in classifying human nature into types and making generalisations about them. This is the neo-classical interpretation of the passage, and there is some evidence in the *Poetics* to support it (for example the important statement at 36.30). But Aristotle had laid it down in set terms that tragedy is not an imitation of character, but of doings (25.11); his starting-point is not psychology, but myth. In Chapter 9 'universal' appears to mean 'consistent with common observation and experience' rather than 'consistent with the fable as a whole'; though what is the second may and indeed should also be the first. But we cannot safely assume Aristotle to mean more than that the statements of poetry form part of a consistent whole, whereas those of history are a mere collection of unrelated facts. From a different starting-point, Coleridge's distinction between the 'unifying' imagination and the 'aggregating' fancy exactly parallels Aristotle's distinction between the *universal* and the *particular*. (See Index, p. 93, under 'Universal').

4. PROBABILITY

Wholeness is closely connected in the *Poetics* with Probability, which is a much looser, and perhaps an ambiguous, concept. Aristotle almost always combines Probability with Necessity; which gives a clue to its meaning. The earliest reference in the *Poetics* to these two notions, in Chapter 7, does not actually contain Aristotle's word for probability. He has defined a 'whole' as that which has a beginning, a middle, and an end; and he defines an end as 'that which naturally (either of necessity or *most commonly*) follows something else' (27.14–15). But later in the same chapter he describes the whole structure as 'a chain of *probability* or necessity' (28.6). Here he is referring to the logical connexion between things, and this seems to be the leading thought in his concept of probability. It is clearly expressed in Chapter 15, when he says the characters should 'say or do such things as it is necessary or probable that they would, being what they are', and that in the plot 'for this to follow that' should be either necessary or probable (37.15–18). This is what he appears to mean at the beginning of Chapter 9, when he says it is the poet's business to tell 'the kind of things that would happen— what is possible according to probability or necessity' (29.3–6). He slightly confuses the issue by his use of the word 'possible', which he sometimes practically identifies with 'probable' and sometimes sharply contrasts with it (e.g. in the paradox with which he was so pleased that he put it into the *Poetics* twice, 'Probable impossibilities are to be preferred to unconvincing possibilities': 54.17–18 and 58.19–21). But the real distinction is not between the probable and the possible, but between the probable and the actual, as at the beginning of Chapter 9.

A more serious confusion is between two kinds of probability, the philosophical and the merely statistical: this second seems to be indicated in the phrase from Chapter 7 quoted at the beginning of this note. And Aristotle's conception of probability deteriorates rather quickly in Chapter 9. When he says that comic fables are plotted on a base of probabilities (29.20–1), he must surely be referring to the stock situations which began to develop in the comedy of his contemporaries; and his explanation of the different practice in tragedy (29.23–8), though ingenious and founded on a shrewd observation, seems to identify probability even more closely with *common knowledge*. Because of this ambiguity, the doctrine of probability has been interpreted very differently at different times.

Aristotle himself understood the difference between the looser and the stricter use of the word. He gives a definition in the *Rhetoric* (Book 1, Chapter 2): 'Probability is what usually happens, *but not merely that* ...; it is analogous to universality.' Elsewhere in the *Rhetoric* he quotes Agathon's epigram, twice referred to in the *Poetics* (43.5–6; 58.26), and explains it thus: 'Improbabilities happen, therefore the improbable is also probable. But not absolutely; as in casuistry fallacies arise when you neglect the circumstances of a proposition, and to whom you are applying it, and in what manner, so improbability cannot be absolutely probable, but *only in certain instances*' (*Rhet.* II. 24). For example (43.2–3): it is not probable that a clever man should be outwitted; but it is probable that a *wicked* clever man should over-reach himself. Most likely Aristotle read more into Agathon's epigram than that poet intended.

D. AESTHETIC VALUES

There are two sets of values running through the *Poetics*: the fundamental values that make poetry more philosophical than history, and the pragmatic values that make one poem succeed where another fails. Aristotle himself draws this distinction at the end of Chapter 15 (38.6–8). I group these pragmatic values together under the heading 'aesthetic', because they concern what Aristotle is referring to when he calls a Fable 'beautiful' or 'well formed'; and in order to distinguish this aspect of his theory from the aspects covered by Notes B and C. A good example of his aesthetic approach is the discussion of amplitude in Chapter 7 (27.20–28.8): the general rule is 'the fuller the more beautiful, so long as the outline remains clear'. But inevitably the two sets of values often overlap or combine; as in his remarks about colour and form in painting (20.32–21.5, 26.6–9).

1. CHARACTER AND MORALITY

Aristotle's approach to character in poetry contrasts sharply with Plato's. To Plato, character is the end of imitative poetry; it exists in order to depict people, and if it is tolerated at all it must depict the kind of person we should like to emulate. To Aristotle, character only comes into poetry because you cannot have fiction without depicting people; and the kind of person you depict must depend on the effect you wish to produce by your fable. His analysis of character in poetry is therefore controlled by aesthetic rather than moral principles; and when he speaks of character or 'the characters' he is usually speaking about *characterization*, and not necessarily generalizing about human nature. There is no great danger of going wrong about this if one takes each remark in its context.

But Aristotle no less than Plato conceived character primarily in terms of goodness and badness; in fact, one and the same word in Greek does duty for both character and morals. Most modern readers would flatly disagree with the statement that 'all men differ in character according to their degree of goodness or badness' (19.1–2); we tend to judge a man not so much by his propensities as by what he makes of them. Aristotle's definition of Character in Chapter 6 is 'what shows a man's disposition— the kind of things he chooses or rejects when his choice is not obvious' (26.17–19); with this we should be less likely to disagree, but we should think it only a part of character— the moral part. The sense of the Greek word lies somewhere between 'character' and 'morals'; the old word 'manners' (as in William of Wykeham's motto, 'Manners maketh Man') would be just right, if its meaning had not so sadly degenerated since the seventeenth century.[1] In reading any modern translation of the *Poetics* it is necessary to know, and constantly to remember, that 'character' always bears this moral sense. Much of what we include in character Aristotle classed as Thought—see Note B, p. 66; in Chapter 6 he says that a man's individuality is determined by his Character *and Thought* (24.20–1).

A corollary of this moral bias is that the traditional Greek morality was relative. A man's character is measurable by its position on the moral scale; or (pragmatically speaking) by how much weight people assign to his acts and his possible acts. It is significant that Aristotle prefers to speak in comparatives, as at 19.2–5, 10–13, and 16–17. The distinction he draws between tragedy and comedy in

[1] It is in the old, undegenerate, sense that Ben Jonson and Dryden use the word 'manners' in their critical writings.

this last passage is that the persons (and as he afterwards says, the events) of tragedy *matter* more, and those of comedy less. Dionysus in the *Bacchae* of Euripides is not 'good' in our sense of the word (he is treacherous and cruel), but he is formidable; the same god in the *Frogs* of Aristophanes is not particularly bad, but he is undignified and ineffective.

There is a special word in Greek to convey this kind of 'goodness': the word SPOUDAIŎTĒS, which Matthew Arnold misleadingly rendered 'high seriousness'. There is no parallel word in English; I have taken 'of high value' for my normal rendering, to indicate that the standard it applies is both relative and pragmatic. I give below examples of the use of this word in the *Poetics*, arranging them roughly so as to begin with the simplest:

23.9–10: 'there are no early records of comedy, because it was not *highly valued*'.

23.28–30: 'any one who can tell a tragedy *of high value* from a poor one can do the same for an epic'.

56.21–3: 'In making moral judgements of a speech or action, you must consider not only the statement or act itself, to see whether it is *good* or bad...'.

44.5–7: 'A man's knowledge or ignorance of these matters is irrelevant to the *serious* censure of his poetry'.

18.28–9: 'the people in the imitation must be either *high* or low'. Cf. p. 19, l. 28 and p. 23, l. 21.

24.4–5: 'Tragedy is an imitation of an action *of high importance*'.

29.12–13: 'poetry is more philosophical and *of higher value* than history'.

But most of Aristotle's words for good and bad can be taken more easily; the Greeks were particularly rich in such words. The discussion of what I have called 'The Tragic Pattern', in Chapter 13 (**33**.10–34.2), illustrates the subtlety with which they distinguished between different kinds and degrees of goodness and badness. This passage also shows how Aristotle's approach to characterization was aesthetic rather than moral: he is discussing what will *produce the technically finest tragedy* (34.9–10).

His requirements in Chapter 15 are more fundamental. The principle of 'wholeness'—see Note C, pp. 71–3—accounts for consistency; that of 'high importance', for goodness; the purgation of fear, for lifelikeness (cf. 33.19–20); 'probability', for appropriateness. Unfortunately the exact meaning of 36.31–37.2 is obscured by a corruption in the Greek text; I have accepted Vahlen's emendation, which has the merits of being closer to the manuscripts than Bywater's and giving a better sense. I do not believe that Aristotle would have made the silly statement that it is inappropriate in a woman to be brave or clever; especially as it conflicts with several famous examples in Greek tragedy and epic—for instance Homer's Penelope, Aeschylus's Clytemnestra, Sophocles's Antigone, and Euripides's Medea. But he may well have said that there are *kinds* of courage and cleverness that are unnatural in a woman. By ill luck the two examples he gives of inappropriateness (37.9–11) are from lost works, and it is idle to draw inferences from them.

2. MODE; SENSATIONALISM, THE CRISIS OF FEELING

Greek music and to some extent Greek literature were modal; that is to say they were canalized into kinds according to the particular psychological effect aimed at. Aristotle sees the division of drama into tragedy and comedy as a modal division; and in the definition of tragedy he specifies the mode of tragedy ('by means of pity and fear effecting its purgation of these emotions': 24.7–8). Much of what he says in the *Poetics* depends on this interpretation of the tragic mode; especially the passage in Chapter 9 concerning sensationalism (30.16–31).

He begins this passage by complaining that even good poets put too much strain on their plots in order to provide their actors with sensational scenes; but he then reflects that sensationalism serves a legitimate purpose in tragedy— it evokes pity and fear—(he afterwards, in Chapter 24, went so far as to say that sensational matter *must* be included in tragedies: 53.32). This leads him to the further reflexion that a sensation is heightened when it is not only unexpected but also probable, or even when it is only apparently probable. The passage deserves close study as an example of Aristotle's powers of rapid constructive thinking, and also of his ability to co-ordinate aesthetic with more fundamental considerations.

His requirement that tragedies should contain a Crisis of Feeling (see Note C, p. 71) is another modal requirement. This detail in his theory of tragedy has not received as much attention as its importance warrants.

3. UNHAPPY ENDING. TRAGIC ERROR

Several of Aristotle's secondary requirements or desiderata for tragedy depend on his definition of the tragic mode.

He assumes in Chapter 6 that tragedy is an imitation of happiness (25.11–12), and at the end of Chapter 7 that a tragic action should contain a change from misfortune to good fortune or from good fortune to misfortune (28.4–8). The word for happiness is EUDAIMŎNIĀ; both the Greek and the English word originally mean 'doing well' in the widest and fullest sense, though in popular usage their meanings diverge, the Greek towards success or even wealth, and the English towards contentment or com- placency. But when Aristotle says that tragedy imitates happiness, all he means is that a tragic action involves the welfare of all the persons participating in it; only so can it evoke pity and fear in the spectator's mind.

The 'unhappy ending' is no part of Aristotle's definition of tragedy; nor could it have been, since Greek tragedies did not necessarily so end. But in Chapter 13 he argues his way methodically to the conclusion that in a well-formed tragedy there should be no change from misfortune to good fortune. Later criticism has on the whole endorsed his judgement, and it is the more to his credit since the happy ending was in favour in his day; he tells us that critics went so far as to censure Euripides because *many* of his plays end in misfortune (34.10–12). Nor does he fall into the opposite error, exposed by Dr Johnson in his Preface to Shakespeare, of thinking that a happy ending can turn tragedy into comedy; he merely remarks that the pleasure derived from that kind of ending is proper to comedy (34.23–7).

It is in the course of this argument in Chapter 13 that Aristotle introduces into his theory a detail of which later critics have made too much: the 'tragic error'. He is giving an incidental warning to tragic dramatists not to be too moral. If the persons in a play are faultless, the disaster will not evoke pity or fear, but only disgust; and if they are utterly evil, it will leave us cold, since, as Aristotle shrewdly observes, nobody puts himself in that class ('pity is induced by undeserved misfortune, and *fear by the misfortunes of normal people*': 33.18–20). Since, then, the disaster must be undeserved and yet not 'disgusting', there is no appropriate cause left for it but a *false step*—either by going astray, or by stumbling in the right path. The Greek word used by Aristotle is HAMARTIA. This false step does not necessarily proceed from a defect of character, or even a miscalculation; through no fault of his own a man may be in a position where he must make one of two errors, and he may be the more tragic for choosing the 'right' one—as Orestes did in the *Choëphori*, and Antigone in the play named after her. HAMARTIA should therefore not be rendered either 'error *of judgement*' or 'flaw' (in character). The theory of the 'tragic flaw' belongs rather to the Christian era and to a certain phase of Shakespearean criticism. It does not fit the facts very well, and even if it did it is not Aristotle's theory (see Chapter 6, p. 25, ll. 13–15: 'it is their characters that give men their quality, but *their doings that make them happy or the opposite*'). It may have arisen because in the Greek New Testament HAMARTIA is the regular word for 'sin'.

4. IRONY OF EVENTS AND DISCLOSURE

In Chapter 6 Aristotle singles out *Irony of events* (PERI-PETEIA) and *Disclosure* (ANAGNORISIS) as 'the chief means by which tragedy moves us' (25.31–2). But neither of them is essential; 'simple' tragedies dispense with both (31.3–6).

PERIPETEIA is commonly rendered 'Reversal of Fortune'. But it is more than a mere change from one state to the opposite; that constitutes a 'simple' action. It is when the movement is *first one way and then the other* that we get what Aristotle calls a 'complex' fable: the two examples in the first paragraph of Chapter 11 (31.15–21) make his meaning quite clear. As Margoliouth and F. L. Lucas have pointed out, he has in mind what we call the Irony of Fate. It is the coming full circle of a wheel, which first carries a man up and then down; and it is linked closely with the primitive but persistent idea of 'pride before a fall', which, not only in Greek drama but ever since, has been one of the most important channels of tragedy. But it can also work the other way, from misfortune to good fortune ('the darkest hour before the dawn'), as in Aristotle's second example.

Disclosure, as it happens, has played a more important part in the comic tradition. Aristotle's elaborate analysis in Chapter 16 of this convenient device for complicating a story seems to be out of proportion to its significance in the theory of tragedy; but Sophocles was fond of it, and used it very skilfully for tragic purposes. It is simply the revelation of unknown facts, or the clearing up of factual misunderstandings. There is no reason to think it includes the sudden flashes of discernment that we associate with tragedy (e.g. Lear's 'I have ta'en Too little thought of this', or Ferdinand's 'Cover her face. Mine eyes dazzle. She died young' in Webster's *Duchess of Malfi*).

E. REFERENCES TO GREEK LITERATURE AND DRAMA IN THE *POETICS*

I

It is a signal merit of the *Poetics* that Aristotle amply illustrates his generalizations with examples from Greek poetry. Unfortunately many of his references are to poems that have perished, and therefore they only help us to understand his notions when he himself provides his own commentary on them. But some of the poems to which he refers have survived; and the examples he draws from them are occasionally valuable and always interesting.

All educated Greeks at that time knew the Homeric poems at least as well as our forefathers knew the Bible, and Aristotle assumes that degree of knowledge in his examples from Homer, which are often bare references, sometimes to passages of considerable length. Before attacking the *Poetics*, it is a great advantage to have read the whole *Odyssey* in an easy modern translation such as Mr E. V. Rieu's extremely readable version in the 'Penguin Classics'. To Aristotle, Homer was the supreme master of the art of fiction; he says more about him than about any other Greek poet, and any one studying the *Poetics* in detail will want to have at hand translations of both the *Iliad* and the *Odyssey*.

Two plays, the *Oedipus Rex* of Sophocles (or *Oedipus Tyrannus*, 'King Oedipus') and the *Iphigeneia in Tauris* of Euripides ('Iphigeneia among the Taurians'), interested Aristotle particularly, in different ways, because of their plots. (He refers to them simply as the 'Oedipus' and the 'Iphigeneia'). He also makes two interesting criticisms on the plot of the *Medea* of Euripides. An English reader who knows these three plays will have some idea of the range of tragedy as it appeared to Aristotle, and will understand the *Poetics* the better; the *Iphigeneia*, for example, will introduce him to a kind of play Aristotle had to allow for in his theory of tragedy, whereas we should probably exclude it from the class.

The other surviving plays he refers to are the *Choëphori* of Aeschylus, the *Antigone* and *Electra* of Sophocles, and the *Orestes* and *Iphigeneia at Aulis* of Euripides.

2

Few readers who do not know Greek will want to investigate closely Aristotle's remarks about the detail of particular plays or poems. But I give below short notes on some of the more important general or particular references to Greek literature in the *Poetics*. I have ignored all except a few of the references to poems that have not survived, nor have I commented on illustrations that seem to me to explain themselves. Any one who wants a full commentary on the particular allusions in the *Poetics* can find one in Sir William Hamilton Fyfe's edition in the Loeb Classical Library (1927), or in the same writer's edition of Bywater's translation (Clarendon Press, 1940). For general information it is sufficient to refer to a reliable English encyclopedia or dictionary; for more specialized knowledge, to the *Oxford Classical Dictionary*.

17.8: *dithyramb*. Originally a song by a company of revellers, with traditional words, to an improvised tune. In its developed form it was an ode in stanzas, sung to an instrumental accompaniment by a trained choir with a leader, who might also be the composer-poet. Dryden's *Alexander's Feast* is an imitation dithyrambic poem.

18.2: *the farces of Sophron and Xenarchus*. The point is that they were in prose. The Greek name for these plays is MIMOS, but as modern miming is a silent art I have avoided the word 'mime'.

18.2–3: *Socratic dialogues*. Not written by Socrates, but philosophical dialogues in which a fictitious Socrates was the principal speaker. Several writers besides Plato produced these imaginary conversations.

18.21: *nomic poetry*. In Aristotle's time this kind of poem was not substantially different from the dithyramb (see note on **17**.8), but nomic verse was continuous, not in stanzas.

20.8: *Chionides and Magnes*. The earliest *Athenian* comic dramatists whose names Aristotle knew. Only a few fragments of their plays have survived.

21.19: '*Margites*'. A celebrated burlesque epic, which has not survived.

22.10: *leaders of the dithyramb*. See note on **17**.8.

22.21: *satyr-drama*. Grotesque plays, so called because the chorus represented satyrs. These plays have no historical connexion with satire, which was a Roman invention named with a Latin word meaning 'hotch-potch'. The satyr-plays survived side by side with tragedy. Aristotle supposes that they were the descendants of the primitive song and dance out of which drama developed, and the ancestors of tragedy.

23.17: *Epicharmus*. See 20.7. Nothing is known of Phormis, who was presumably, like Epicharmus, a Sicilian and an older contemporary of Chionides and Magnes.

Crates. About the middle of the fifth century; a contemporary of Sophocles.

29.19: *comedy*. Aristotle is referring to the 'Middle Comedy', which flourished in his time, and of which only small fragments have survived. What he says only partly applies to the Old Comedy; Aristophanes mixed caricatures of his contemporaries with purely fictitious characters. But according to Aristotle the decisive step was from the old lampooners to the earliest comic writers: see Chapter 4 (21.20–30) and Chapter 5 (23.16–19).

29.31: *Agathon*. The latest of the celebrated fifth-century tragic dramatists of Athens, forty years younger than Euripides though he only outlived him by four or five years. All his plays have perished.

31.18: *the 'Lynceus'*. By Theodectes, a contemporary of Aristotle's. Cf. 41.24–7, where Abas is called 'the boy'.

34.11: *Euripides*. This is interesting, since several of his 'tragedies' (including the *Iphigeneia in Tauris*) have happy endings. But he seems to have become more tragic towards the end of his life, whereas Sophocles (like Shakespeare) seems to have preferred 'double' fables in his latest period.

34.26: *Aegisthus*. The enemy of Agamemnon, who was afterwards killed by Orestes. See the *Choëphori* of Aeschylus, the *Electra* of Sophocles, or the *Electra* of Euripides.

37.9: *the 'Orestes'*—of Euripides.

37.20: *Medea*. She is rescued from Jason at the end of the play by divine intervention.

37.20–1: *Book 2 of the 'Iliad'*. The Greek army mutiny and are about to sail away, but the goddess Athene makes Odysseus stop them.

38.19–21 : *Odysseus, the nurse, and the herdsmen*. In *Odyssey*, Book 19, ll. 335–475, and Book 21, ll. 188–224.

39.9: *'Choëphori'*. The 'Libation-bearers' of Aeschylus. This and the next example (from a proposed improvement of the *Iphigeneia in Tauris*—cf. 41.1–3) are sufficient to explain 'Disclosure by logic'.

39.21–2: '*Odysseus disguised as a Messenger*'. In this lost play (as in the *Odyssey*) the suspense was clearly prolonged by an unexpected postponement of the disclosure. When Odysseus strung the bow, the suitors were too infatuated (or drunk) to draw the obvious conclusion.

40.11: *Amphiaraüs*. As the play is lost it is impossible to say exactly what was wrong; but in Chapter 24 (**54.1–4**) Aristotle gives a clear example of the kind of thing he has in mind.

40.25–41.8: *the 'Iphigeneia'*. The reader can judge the merits of this analysis by comparing it with the play. In l. 31, the *reason* was the madness, and the *purpose* the purification; according to Aristotle these are not essential to the fable, but they are 'correct' interpolations.

41.24–7: *the 'Lynceus' of Theodectes*. The Greek text of the later part of this sentence is corrupt, and cannot be interpreted with certainty in the absence of the play; but see **31.18–21**. (The modern use of the word *dénouement* does not correspond exactly to Aristotle's definition in ll. 19–24 of the 'untying of the knot', which may begin at the very beginning of the play.)

42.3: *the 'Prometheus'*. Not the *Prometheus Bound* of Aeschylus, but a lost play.

54.16: *Book 19 of the 'Odyssey'*. The untrue story told by Odysseus to Penelope (ll. 164–307). Aristotle is advocating the introduction of what Pooh-Bah called 'corroborative detail, intended to give artistic verisimilitude to an otherwise bald and unconvincing narrative'.

54.23: *the 'Electra'*—of Sophocles. The extravagance here consists in an anachronism.

54.30: *the landing on Ithaca*. Book 13, ll. 113–25.

56.14–15: *Xenophanes*. A sixth-century philosopher-poet. He was perhaps the first distinguished Greek writer to raise the objection with which we are familiar from Plato's *Republic*.

57.5–10: '*The others, gods and men. . . .*' The crucial word 'all' does not occur in Aristotle's quotation; but it is clearly implied. The reference is to the opening lines of Book 10 of the *Iliad*. If this was a stock criticism in Aristotle's day, their text must have differed from ours, which says 'The other *Achaean chieftains* slept all night long in their tents'; this of course is consistent with any amount of noise in the *Trojan* camp.

57.13–15: *Hippias the Thasian's proposals.* (*a*) In Greek, as in several other languages, the sense of a word often varied according to the way it was accented. Thus in the first example, Hippias turned a statement ('We promise') into a command ('Promise') by moving the accent from the first to the second syllable of DIDOMEN. Here, as at 5–6, the text to which Aristotle refers differed from our text of the *Iliad*; but I give the reference as to his text. (*b*) The Greeks had no letter corresponding to our 'h'; the difference, for example, between OMER and HOMER was simply a matter of pronunciation, marked in writing by two different phonetic symbols above the initial vowel. A scribe could easily mistake the sense of a passage and alter it drastically by adding or removing the aspirate; as here, where it makes the difference between two almost opposite statements.

59.4: *Aegeus.* In the *Medea*.

59.5: *Menelaus in the 'Orestes'.* See **37.**9, and note on p. 85.

INDEX

(References to Introduction and Notes are in italic figures)

I. TOPICS AND CRITICAL VOCABULARY

Accident, accidental, 5, 30, 51, 67

Action, *see* Doing

Actors, 19, 22, 24, 25, 27, 30, 32, 43, 53, 54, 59, 60, *68*; act (vb), 20, 24, 40; 'the performer's art', 44, 60

Affection and enmity, 31; (family) affections, *35*

Allegory, *7*

Ambiguity, *57*

Amplitude, 22, 24, 27–8, *75*; length, 23, 41, 51, 60; size, 27, *52*

Anachronism, *86*

Appropriateness, 26, 27, 36–7, 50, *53, 78*

Art, 17, 27, 28, 55, 59, *67*; artistic, *35*; inartistic, *38*

Audience, *6*, 34, 39, 40, 53, 59

Beauty, beautiful, well formed, fine, 17, 26, 27, 28, 30, 33, 34, 50, 52, *75, 80*; refinements, *35, 38*

Beginning, middle, and end, *4*, 27, 51, *73*

Blunders, 40, 53, 54, 58

Casuistry, *74*

Catastrophe, 31

Character, morality, *75–8.* Character, *9, 11*, 17, 18–19, 21, 24, 25, 26, 36–8, *53, 55, 63, 75*; moral: (actions), 36; (speeches), 25, 36; (epics), 52; (tragedies), 42; non-moral: (personages), 53; (portraits) 25; (speeches),

26; (tragedies), 25; morality, *80*; immorality, 59. Characterization, 26, *75, 78*; low characters, lack of dignity, 37, 59. *See also* People; Politics

Chorus, 22, 32, 43

Christianity and paganism, *11*

Clearness, *see* Language

Comedy, 17, 18, 19, 20, 21, 22, 23, 24, 29, 34, *63–4, 66, 74, 76–7, 78, 80, 82, 85*; comic mask, 23

Completeness, *see* Unity

Complexity and simplicity, *see* Fable

Consistency, 7, *11*, 37, *78*; inconsistency, 58, 59

Context, 58

Conversation, 22, 50, 51

Conviction, *see* Probability

Correctness, rightness, 55; incorrectness, 59

Crisis of feeling, *see* Emotion

Customary usage, 57

Dance, dancers, ballet, *10*, 17, 19, 22, 53, 60, *68*

Deformity, 23

Dénouement, *see* Tying and untying of the knot

Deus ex machina, 37

Dialogue, speeches, 19, 22, 25, 26, 40, 43

Dignity, *see* Character

Disclosure, revelation, 25, 31–2, 36, 38–40, 40–1, *52, 81, 82, 85*

Disgust, disgusting, bad taste, 33, 36, *80*

Dithyramb, dithyrambic poetry, 17, 18, 19, 22, 51, *84*

Doings, action, experiences, *70-1*. Doing, doings, *11*, 17, 18, 21, 24, 25, 28, 30, 32, *66*, *72*, *81*; action, *4*, 24, 25, 26, 27, 28, 30, 31, 32, 51, 56, 60; incidents, 24, 25, 26, 27, 30, 35, 36, 37, 41, 43, 56; experiences, 17, 32, *67*

Drama, dramatic, *10*, 19, 20, 21, 51, 53, 59, *67*

Elements of poetry, 17, 23, 24-5, 32, 41, 42, 52

Emotion, feelings, 24, 26, 40, 43, *63*, *64*, *67*, *71*; crisis of feeling, emotional crisis, 32, 36, 52, *71*, *79*; emotional: (tragedies), 41-2; (epics), 52

End (1) = reason for a thing's existence, *8*, *10*, 25, 51, 55-6, 60, 61

(2), *see* Beginning, middle, and end; *also under* Happiness and unhappiness

Epic (1): *11*, 17, 22, 23, 41, 51-4, 59-61,*68-9*; 'the art that uses prose, or verse without music', 19, *68*; 'the art that imitates in hexameters', 24; 'the poetry that imitates in narrative verse', 51. Kinds of epic, 52; elements of epic, 23, 52

(2): in the sense of 'multi-fabular', or 'combining several actions', 42, 60

(3) Epic metre = hexameter: *see under* Verse and prose

Episode (1) Act (EPEISODION) = the main divisions of a play, 22, 32

(2) Episodic actions, 30; interpolation of episodes, 40-1, 52, 53

Error: (comic), 23; (tragic),33-4, *80-1*

Essence, essential,*9*, 24, 55,*69*

Etymology, 20

Experience, trial and error, 17, 53

Extravagance, extravagant incidents, 37, 53, 54, 58, 59

Fable (MYTHOS) (1): *10-11*, 22, 23, 24, 25-6, 27-32, 33-6, 37, 38-41, 42-3, 54, 60, *63*, *69-74*. Simple and complex fables, 31, 33, *81*; simple: (stories), 42; (epics), 52; (tragedies), 52; complex: (tragedies), 41; (epics), 52. Single and double fables, 33, 70; double: (plots), 34; (fables), *85*

(2) Myth: *11*, *70*,*72*; 'the traditional fables', 30, 35; 'the fables', 36

Fallacies, *see* Logic

Farces, 18, *84*

Fatalism, *11*

Fate, fated, 39, *81*

Fear, *see* Pity and fear

Fiction, 7, *9*, *65*, 75 *et passim*

Force, 17, 26, 27, *67*

General, generic, *see* Universal

Genius, 40, 51

Happiness and unhappiness, good fortune and misfortune, 24, 25, 28, 31, 32, 33, 41, *66*, *79-80*, *81-2*; unhappy ending to tragedy, *2*, 34, *80*

High value, importance (SPOU-DAIOTES), 77; 'high', 18, 19, 21, 23; 'of high value', 23,

29; 'highly valued', 23; 'high importance', 24, *78*; 'good' (speech or action), 56; 'serious' (censure of poetry), 44; 'studiously serious' (Sidney), *4*; 'high seriousness' (Arnold), 77

History, *4*, 29, 51, *72*, 75

Human feeling, 43; humane, 33

Imagination, *10*, 40

Imitation (MIMESIS), *3*, *5*, *9–10*, 17–21, 24, 25, 28, 30, 31, 33, 35, 37, 53, 55, 59, 60, *65–8*, *75 et passim*; representation, *5*, *7*, *9*, 20. Medium of imitation, 17–18, 24, 25, *68–9*; object of imitation, 17, 18–19, 24, 25, *66*; manner of imitation, 17, 19, 25

Importance, *see* High value

Impossibility, *see* Possibility

Improvisation, 21, 22

Incidents, *see* Doings

Interpolation, *see* Episode (2)

Intonation, 22, 45

Irony of events (PERIPETEIA), 25, 31, 32, 38, 42, 52, *81–2*; ironical plots, 41

Lampoons, lampooners, 21, 22, 23, 29

Language, *9*, 17, 22, 24, 25, 26, 43, 44–51, 52, 54, 55, 56–8, *63*, *68*; clearness of language, 48, 49

Laughter, 23, *63*

Learning, knowledge, *5*, 20

Life, *12*, 25, *67*, 70

Lifelikeness, 37, 40, *78*; 'living [a story] oneself', *10*, 19, 40

Logic, logical, *3*, *13*, 30, 39, *73*; fallacies, 39, 54, 58, *74*

Lyrical poetry, *67*

Madness, 40

Magic, *10*

Manners, *76*

Masks, 23

Melodrama, *70*

Metaphor, 46–7, 48–9, 50–1, 53, 55, 57

Metre, metres, *see* Verse and prose

Mise en scène, 24, 25, 26–7, 34–5, 52, 60; scene-painting, scenery, 22, *68*

Mode, *78–9*

Monotony, 53

Morality, moral, non-moral, immoral. *See* Character

Music, 17, 21, 60, *63*, *67*, *68*, *78*; melody, 18, 24, *25*, 26, 52; flute and lyre art, 17, 19; flute-players, 59; pipes, 17; singers, 60

Myth, *see* Fable

Narrative, narration, narrate, *10*, 19, 23, 24, 51, 53, 67

Naturalism, *7*

Nature, natural, naturally, *3*, *4*, *5*, *9*, 20, 21, 22, 24, 27, 28, 40, 53

Nome, nomic poetry, 18, 19, *84*

Parodies, 19

People, persons, men, 24, 25, 26, 33–4, *75*; normal, above the norm, or below it, 18–19, 33, 37, *80*; illustrious or low, 21, lower types 23; better or worse, 34; 'conspicuous', 'of high degree', *2*, 33

Peripeteia, peripety, *see* Irony of events

Phallic performances, 22

Philosophers, philosophical, *4*, *5*, *11*, *12*, 20, 29, *74*, 75

Phonetics, 44, 45, 57

Pity and fear, 24, 30, 32, 34–5, 43, 78, 80; fearful and pitiful events, 33; fear, 31, 78, terrible experiences and doings, 34

Plastic arts, 65; colour and outline, 17; works of art, 20; painters, painting, pictures, 26, 27, 51, 75; portraits, portrait-painters, 21, 25, 37, 58

Pleasure, delight, 5, 20–1, 30, 34, 35, 43, 51, 54, 60, 61, 63

Plot (SYSTASIS), structure (SYNTHESIS). Plot, 28, 34, 52, 53, 54, 69, 79; plotting of incidents, fables, poems, putting together fables, 17, 25, 26, 27, 29, 33–5, 36, 37, 40, 51, 60; 'plotted tragedies', 34. Structure, 24, 27, 31, 33, 69

Poetic licence, 58

Poets, 6, 9, 10, 34, 38, 47, 51, 53, 55 et passim

Politics (=social morality), 26, 55

Popularity, 59

Possibility, 29, 30, 73–4; impossibility, 54, 55, 58, 59

Probability and necessity, 11, 28, 29, 30, 31, 37, 'likelihood or necessity'(Sidney), 4; 'either of necessity or most commonly', 27, 73; probability, 5, 39–40, 73–4, 79; conviction, 29, 40; probable (convincing) impossibilities, 54, 58; probable improbabilities, 43, 58, 74

Prologues, 23, 32, 53

Prose, see Verse and prose

Psychology, 6, 13, 72, 78

Published works of Aristotle, 38, 62

Purgation, 24, 63, 64, 78

Rhapsodies, rhapsodes, 18, 60

Rhetoric, 26, 43, 66, 67

Rhythm, 17, 18, 21, 24

Satire, 84

Satyr-drama, satyr-poetry, 22, 84

Scenery, see Mise en scène

Science, scientists, scientific, 5, 13, 18, 44, 55, 56; medicine, 18; physiology, 55

Self-expression, 10, 67

Sensationalism, 30, 53–4, 79; use of the mise en scène to startle, 35

Significance, see Universal

Sin, 81

Socratic dialogues, 18, 84

Stage, 22, 27, 42, 53, 54, 60; theatrical: (effect), 30; (performances), 34, 40

Standard words, 46, 48, 50

Structure, see Plot

Theatre, see Stage; Audience

Thought, 24, 25, 26, 43, 52, 55, 66, 76

Tradition, 56, 58

Tragedy passim. Definition, 24; development, 22; elements, 24–5; enhancing beauties, 24, 26; the four kinds, 41–2, 52; the tragic mode, 78; 'imitation by means of actors', 51

Tying and untying of the knot, 41, 42, untying of the fable, 37, 'an intrigue perplexed and unravelled' (Johnson), 4; dénouement, 86

Unfair fault-finding, 42; wrong criticism, 34, 58

Unhappy ending, see Happiness and unhappiness

Unities, the Three, *2*

Unity, unit, completeness, wholeness, the whole, *3*, 24, 27, 28-9, 30, 46, 51, 60, *71, 73, 78*

Universal (KATHOLOU), *71-3*; universality, *74*; universalisation and particularisation, 29, (Sidney), *4*; unification and aggregation (Coleridge), *72-3*; unified: (stories), 23, (actions), 60; significant and unified outline, 40; significant opinions, 26; 'general' and 'particular' (Arnold), *5*; 'general' and 'individual' (Wordsworth), *5*; 'generic' and 'individual' (Coleridge), *5*

Untrue stories, 54

Verse and prose, 17, 26, 29, *68-9*; verse, verses, metre, metrical speech, 18, 23, 24, 30. Metres, 17-18, 21, 53; elegiac, 18; hexameter (or 'epic', or 'heroic', metre), 18, 21, 22, 24, 51, 53, 60, *68*; iambic (trimeters), 18, 21, 22, 51, 53; trochaic (tetrameters), 22, 53

Vividness, *10*, 40, 60

Women, 36-7, 60, *78*

2. NAMES AND TITLES

(a) *Greek*

(In this section only references of particular interest or to well-known persons or works are given. Titles of works are shown in italics under the name of the author.)

Aeschylus, 22, 42, 50, *78*; *Choëphori*, 39, *81, 85*

Agathon, *38*, 42, 43, *74, 85*; *Anthos*, 29

Alcibiades, 29

Alexander the Great, *12*

Aristophanes, 19, *85*; *Frogs*, 77

Aristotle, *Politics*, *63*, 64, 67; *Rhetoric*, *13*, 43. 74

Athens, *12, 13*, 20, 23

Carcinus, 38, 40

Chaeremon, 18, 53

Demosthenes, *68*

Diogenes Laertius, *1*

Empedocles, 18, 47, 57

Epicharmus, 20, 23

Euripides, *3*, 34, 42, 43, 50, 56, 59, *80, 85*; *Bacchae*, 77; *Iphigeneia at Aulis*, 37; *Iphigeneia in Tauris*, 32, 36, 38, 39, 40, *83, 85, 86*; *Medea*, 35, 37, *78, 83, 87*; *Orestes*, 37, 59

Glaucon, 58

Herodotus, 29

Homer, *11, 13*, 18, 19, 21, 28, 38, 44, 51, 52, 53, 54, 60, 70, *78, 82-3*; 'the Maeonian star', *3*; *Iliad*, 9, 37, 42, 46, 52, 54, 56, 60; *Margites* (attributed to Homer), 21; *Odyssey*, 34, 38, 39, 41, 52, 54, 58, 60, *83, 86*

'Longinus', *4, 67*

Plato, *9*, 10, *12, 13, 68, 75, 76, 84*; *Cratylus*, *9*; *Republic*, *13*, 86

Polygnotus, 19, 25, *58*

INDEX

Polyidus, 39, 41
Protagoras, 44

Sappho, 68
Sicily, 20, 23
Sophocles, 3, 19, 22, 39, 43, 56,
    82, 85; Antigone, 36, 78, 81;
    Electra, 54, 85, 86; Oedipus

Tyrannus 31, 35, 37, 39, 54, 60,
    83
Theodectes, 39, 85; Lynceus, 31, 41

Xenophanes, 56, 86

Zeuxis, 25, 58

(b) Latin and Modern

Arnold, Matthew, 5, 7, 8, 77

Bacon, Francis, 6
Baudelaire, 10
Boileau, 3
Butcher, S. H., 8, 14, 16, 42, 44
Bywater, Ingram, 2, 8, 13, 14, 16,
    17, 23, 24, 26, 30, 31, 37, 38,
    39, 41, 42, 43, 44, 45, 55, 56,
    59, 63, 68, 72, 78

Chaucer, 2
Coleridge, 5, 7, 8, 72
Cooper, Lane, 2, 16, 63

Dryden, 2, 3, 76, 84

Fyfe, W. Hamilton, 16, 84

Gudeman, A., 14

Horace, 1, 3

Italy, 1, 2

Johnson, Samuel, 3-4, 14, 80

Jonson, Ben, 4, 6-7, 8, 76; Timber,
    65
Juvenal, 10

Lucas, F. L., 8, 16, 81

Margoliouth, D. S., 2, 14, 16, 19,
    28, 49, 65, 68, 81
Murray, Gilbert, 16, 62, 70

Pope, 3

Richards, I. A., 6, 8
Rieu, E. V., 83
Ross, W. D., 16, 67
Rostagni, A., 14, 44
Rymer, 3

Shakespeare, 4, 81, 85; King Lear,
    82
Sidney, 4, 6, 7
Spenser, Faerie Queene, 7

Vahlen, J., 78

Webster, Duchess of Malfi, 82
Wordsworth, 4, 5, 67